EBURY PRESS
THIS HANDMADE LIFE

Nandita Iyer is the author of two immensely popular books, *Everyday Superfoods* and *The Everyday Healthy Vegetarian*. She is the author of the food blog *Saffron Trail* and the column Double Tested in *Mint Lounge*. She has been featured in and has written for *Vogue, BBC Good Food, Femina* and *India Today*, among other publications. She is a trained singer in Hindustani classical music. You can follow her on Twitter and Instagram @saffrontrail.

T0287543

ADVANCE PRAISE FOR THE BOOK

'For most of humanity's history, the ideal of being interdisciplinary and multiskilled was the default. We are sapiens not just because of our outsized brains. It's because we use our hands and brains to make everything from beautiful art to rockets that leave the solar system. The trend towards ignoring hobbies and focusing on becoming specialists in a rat race is a relic of the industrial revolution. Nandita's beautiful book is a gentle yet persuasive reminder that mindfully making things with your hands is what we need in a world that is obsessed with short-attention-span consumption and instant gratification'—Krish Ashok, author of *Masala Lab*

'Nandita's book brings to life the golden saying in Tamil, "*Kai thozhil onrai karrukkol, kavalai unakkillai ottrukkol* [Learn a craft and live without worries]." This book is a must-read for everyone who wants to be *atmanirbhar* [self-reliant], improve the quality of their lives significantly and live stress-free'—Uma Raghuraman, aka Masterchefmom, author of *My Genius Lunch Box*

'Succinct. Useful. And so very joyful! *This Handmade Life* makes one fall in love with the process of creating from scratch. This is a book you need and not just want'—Rukmini Ray Kadam, author of the award-winning decor blog *Trumatter*

This Handmade Life

7 SKILLS *to* **ENHANCE** *and*
TRANSFORM *your everyday life*

nandita iyer

An imprint of Penguin Random House

EBURY PRESS

USA | Canada | UK | Ireland | Australia
New Zealand | India | South Africa | China

Ebury Press is part of the Penguin Random House group of companies
whose addresses can be found at global.penguinrandomhouse.com

Published by Penguin Random House India Pvt. Ltd
4th Floor, Capital Tower 1, MG Road,
Gurugram 122 002, Haryana, India

First published in Ebury Press by Penguin Random House India 2022

Copyright © Nandita Iyer 2022

ISBN 9780143454588

Typeset in Sabon by MAP Systems, Bengaluru, India

www.penguin.co.in

To Amma and Sumanth

Contents

1. My Journey as a Maker   1
2. Baking   24
3. Spice It Up   80
4. Get Fizzy   124
5. Home-Made Beauty   161
6. Lather Up   194
7. Grow   238
8. Fabric and Fibre Art   270
9. The Business of Handmade   308

Acknowledgements   323

Chapter 1

My Journey as a Maker

'The cure for boredom is curiosity.
There is no cure for curiosity.'
—Dorothy Parker

Many women have such graceful hands, with delicate, long fingers and impeccable nails. I am in awe of them because I have workman hands—short, square nails, fingers not stubby but not slender either, roughened palms and fingertips, which are almost heat-proof.

For as long as I can remember, I have been using my hands to make stuff. I was that exasperating kid making 'chutney' by grinding random leaves and berries plucked from the trees in the colony using two stones, while playing 'house-house' with friends. At home, the restless me was forever making music (not to my grandparents' ears, though) by drumming on every available surface. My maternal grandmother would often give me a stern warning that if I didn't stop these antics, my hands would become rough and manly. I don't think that ever bothered me then, and it doesn't bother me now. I can get the most expensive manicure and ruin it on the way home. I cannot even wait to let the nail paint dry before diving hand-long into my next pet project.

I think I was eight years old, and I had to work on a project for school. Projects in the early 1980s didn't mean researching on the Internet. (My thirteen-year-old son will roll his eyes when he reads this.) It meant using your imagination, channelling it into some form of creativity and bringing your idea to life. Living with grandparents who couldn't be bothered to micromanage my schoolwork, all I could do was ask them to get me some raw materials. If I could find those in the storeroom, all the better. I remember making a building with large sheets of cardboard, with windows, pipes and clothes lines on the outside. The cardboard pieces could not be stuck together with Fevicol so I adapted the design to have grooves, and wedges to go into those grooves in the opposing pieces, quite like the present-day IKEA furniture assembly. One look at some of the other kids' projects and I could tell that their parents have given more than a helping hand. Mine wasn't the best-looking project submitted, and I was rather embarrassed to present that drab-looking building on the verge of collapse to my teachers, but the present me is in love with that child, who did not fear to jump headlong into a project and do something she had no idea about.

As a ten-year-old, I learnt by watching my grandfather fix an iron whose wiring had gone loose.

Each time the iron from the bygone era refused to heat up, I would do exactly what I had seen my grandfather do. It involved opening the plug cover with a screwdriver, loosening the screws that held the three wires, shaving off the outer plastic sheath to expose enough copper wiring, passing each of these wires through the tiny holes and winding it around, then tightening the screws and shutting the cover of the plug. Even as a kid, the satisfaction of bringing a cold iron back to life with this simple two-minute job was strong. Due credit needs to go to my grandparents and parents for not hovering over me or mollycoddling me too much. I don't think the same can be said about me as a mother. I would have a panic attack if my thirteen-year-old fiddled with the innards of any electrical equipment.

Childhood was an endless stream of crafts, greeting cards, art out of stuff that would otherwise be thrown away such as peels, plastic bags, etc. Born hipster! Ideas for such projects in the pre-Internet era would be diligently collected from newspapers, magazines, TV shows (even in my days there would be some interesting DIY-focused shows in the afternoon on the lone TV channel Doordarshan). I clearly recall one very time-consuming and elaborate project that involved cutting milk packets into squares and then turning them into circles by stitching around the border with needle and thread, then pulling it together. Over 100(!!) such circles were needed to create a wall hanging with these combined in a pattern. I'm in awe of the reserves of patience we held in us in those days.

I used to watch my aunts use the hand-cranked Usha sewing machine. I would pester them to teach me to use it. Edges of curtains, kitchen towels and literally anything that could be stitched in a straight line, I was game. My aunt would feed the cloth in a straight line, while I would crank the handle as fast as I could. Seeing a piece of cloth become something useful with my contribution was so much fun.

My sister was born when I was nearly ten. What do you gift your baby sister on her first birthday when you have no access to any pocket money? I managed to find some fabric in the cupboard. All those hours spent chugging at the sewing machine with my aunts gave me the confidence to put my imagination to use on the cloth. My gift to my little sister on her first birthday was a frock I had stitched all by myself.

While it is quite unfair to compare 1970s and 1980s kids with present-day kids, I do wonder how it is that we never managed to get bored despite there being only one tedious channel on TV and no Internet or mobile phones. It seems to me that we were not bored because there were no available streams of entertainment. The expectations from the outside world were naturally low, and we had to do things to keep ourselves occupied and happy.

Spending time on such projects was the perfect way to spend after school time or long holidays. My interest in such activities stemmed from the fact that I was an only child for nearly ten years, living with my grandparents and aunts, with no one of my own age at home to play with. Children in those days didn't need much to be fascinated by. It could be a butterfly or a flower or a piece of cardboard, and they could spend an afternoon over it.

Rajan Chandy, in his essay 'On Boredom and Sense-stimulation'[1] published in the *Journal of Krishnamurti Schools*, explains this beautifully:

> '*It is because the child experiences with its entire being that the everyday world seems so fascinating, even magical, and not the other way around. Adults, in contrast, look forward to some extraordinary event; they wait to be strongly stimulated from the outside before they give their entire attention to anything, and even then they often give only their mind, or they give over only their body to the "here and now". Thus, while for the child even the "ordinary" is magical, for the adult even the "extra-ordinary" rapidly loses its significance.*'

Higher studies took over my life, and there was no time to be 'wasted' on these hobbies.

The chemistry lab in junior college followed by anatomy dissections and surgery in medical college enthralled me. I reconnected with the joy of working with my hands during the anatomy dissection term of my first year in medical college, gory as it may sound. Surgery was hands down my favourite subject in medical college, as it was the ultimate combination of knowledge and dexterity. All I wanted to do was to become a surgeon, but the best of life's plans get waylaid.

---

[1] Chandy, R. (n.d.). '*On Boredom and Sense-stimulation,*' *Journal of the Krishnamurti Schools*, http://www.journal.kfionline.org/issue-2/on-boredom-and-sense-stimulation

Once I moved on from medicine to cooking, it was back to my workhorse hands.

If there's one part of our body we take for granted, it is our hands.

Think about it. Touch, hold, grasp, feel, soothe, express, extend friendship, love, make music—there's just so much our hands do, as compared to our feet, which are just meant for transportation.

According to Aristotle, the hand is the 'tool of tools'.

Our hands perform a staggeringly wide range of actions—as delicate as a vascular surgeon using a needle, as intricate as a musician playing the sitar, or as powerful as a mechanic digging a borewell. Hands are used as our first checkpoint for temperature or texture.

I do believe that hands come with a brain of their own. Or rather, the connection with the brain is so swift and so precise that when you pick up salt to season a dish, your hands know exactly how much salt is required for the dish, even without putting active thought into the process. I am often fascinated at how my hands can pick out an exact quantity of dough, say 30 g plus or minus 2 g, when I want to make rotis. Sometimes, just to check if my hand-brain is working fine, I put the dough ball on the kitchen scales to check. I am always surprised with their effortless accuracy. The hands just know.

* * *

By 2015, I was deeply into cooking, being a food blogger and writer since 2006, but besides that I was also into kitchen gardening, bread baking and soap-making.

These hobbies filled the gaps in my day, allowing me to take breaks from writing in a meaningful way. When friends would tell me that I should be selling my soaps and breads, my standard response was that I wanted some hobbies purely for the joy of them and not for any commercial gain. Creating always gives me more pleasure and fulfilment than consuming.

Over the years, I added more creative projects, such as experimenting with sourdough, fermenting, fabric dyeing and upcycling, to my weekends. As a freelance writer, the distinction between weekdays and weekends is rather blurred. Work is only too happy to spill into the weekend. A freelancer's guilt is real. Out of our own guilt of not having made the most of weekdays, we end up scheduling writing and other work in our weekend calendar. This is also true for a lot of people with full-time careers these days. Reserving time on the weekends for such creative projects is also a way of signalling to our mind that these are days for recreation. Our minds need at least one or two days of sabbath from the usual work routines.

Then the 2020 pandemic year dawned on us. Words like social distancing and lockdown became a part of our everyday vocabulary. Everyone was at home 24/7, making stuff with a vengeance as though it was the only thing that could keep us from getting sucked into the whirlpool of COVID-19 anxiety. That was the time when the idea of *This Handmade Life* made perfect sense. The proposal was sent and approved, and I got started on this journey of documenting and hoping to inspire a whole tribe of makers and joy seekers.

* * *

The Positive Side Effects of Making

One doesn't need to understand the science behind the process of creation to get joy out of the creative process, but once you do understand the science behind it, it all makes complete sense.

There is a gamut of positive side effects to pursuing creative hobbies.

The lockdown- and pandemic-driven restrictions in our lives pushed us towards making a lot of things ourselves, which otherwise we would have bought or outsourced. It also made us realize that all these creative activities can be enjoyable and useful, even healing.

I recently made marmalade from oranges. A bottle of a good quality organic jam can be bought for Rs 500. What it cost me was around Rs 100 worth of ingredients and two and a half hours of my time, plus a lot of elbow grease, stirring the pot regularly over a period of two hours. All for two bottles of jam. You may wonder if it is worth spending so much time and effort on something that can be easily bought, more so if it is not too expensive. The rewards here are often intangible.

Let us try and make sense of what the gains are in pursuing these hobbies.

Become more self-reliant

'*Ne te quaesiveris extra*' is a Latin quote with which American philosopher Ralph Waldo Emerson starts his famous essay 'Self Reliance'.[2] Translated into English it means, 'Do not seek outside of yourself/ look within'. The essay shines light on this concept

---

[2] https://en.wikisource.org/wiki/Essays:_First_Series/Self-Reliance

and explains how it enables us to think independently, embrace our individuality and strive for our goals. Being self-reliant for some of our basic needs can be very feel-good. Not being dependent on a store for something like your daily bread or soap can be freeing and a source of joy. Emerson's essay also talks about not relying on 'things' to feel happiness.

Improve your mental health

Basket weaving was used as occupational therapy to reduce anxiety and physical ailments in soldiers during the First World War.

Almost all of us have our smartphones in our hand or within our hand's reach for all the waking hours of the day. Keeping our hands busy in the garden or making bread keeps us away from our phones. If you have ever dealt with sticky dough, you know that it is not possible to operate the touch screen with doughy fingers. Getting my hands dirty with dough, soil, oils or needle and thread has helped me keep my COVID-19 anxiety under control. All the projects I have shared with you in this book improve the mood and mental well-being. Creating something from scratch activates and engages all the senses and reduces the levels of stress hormones. Hobbies are a natural way to reduce levels of cortisol (sustained high levels of cortisol in the body is damaging to health in multiple ways). A study on substance abuse treatments found that gardening led to reduction in cortisol levels and improved quality of life compared to conventional therapies.

There is a special joy in creating stuff with our hands, be it baking bread, tending to a herb garden or making our own soaps. The satisfaction felt at the end of a project also releases feel-good hormones inducing a feeling of well-being. These are all exercises in self-care.

Bring some eustress to your life

In contrast to how too much screen time can increase stress levels, meaningfully engaging in creative activities generates a positive kind of stress called eustress. This variety of stress injects a bit of thrill and enthusiasm into our mundane daily life. Eustress can also counteract the negative kind of everyday stress that builds from the workplace, relationships, etc.

Put time to good use

During the pandemic, almost all our time was being spent indoors. Apart from work-related activities, time can be spent on creating things that we can use in our daily lives and in developing new hobbies. It is also good to have activities other than mindless scrolling of social media or binge-watching series to fill our free time. Many of these projects are a healthy distraction, an exercise in mindfulness and a meditative use of time, all with something exciting to look forward to in the end.

Feel in control

Making things with our own hands is also a way of feeling in control of at least some aspects of our life when the rest of it seems to be spinning out of control and this is not just during COVID-19. These activities provide small oases of calm amidst the stressors of our daily lives such as exams, deadlines and work pressures.

Get back to your roots

Making things from scratch was the norm in our grandparents' times and earlier, especially if they were a proud bourgeois family like mine. It was a combination of a thrifty lifestyle and not too many options being available. For example, making ghee, savouries, sweets and masalas at home; knitting sweaters, stitching some of the home furnishings and clothes for the kids; making greeting cards for festivals, or repairing our old appliances until they were spoilt beyond repair.

Creating things makes us go back to our roots. Eating food that is fresh, preservative-free and packaging-free, using chemical-free beauty stuff for the skin and hair from the kitchen, giving loved ones handmade gifts and a therapeutic screen-free use of leisure time all take us back to the easy laid-back times of the previous generations.

Embrace a sustainable lifestyle

Upcycling projects like tie-dying an old T-shirt or creating a herb garden out of cracked bowls and cups are fun and useful ways to repurpose things that would otherwise go into the trash. Using cores, peels and seeds of seasonal fruits to make your own vinegars is another excellent way to cut down on kitchen waste. Making your own food, spices, sauces, soaps, face masks and oils cuts down on wasteful packaging to a great extent. It also provides avenues for reusing and recycling, when you reuse glass bottles, old tins or boxes for packaging purposes. Hobbies like kitchen gardening can use up all the kitchen waste as compost. Herbs from the garden can go into making soaps and oils.

Develop a social circle

The best kind of friends are the ones with whom you enjoy doing similar activities. Having a Diwali goodies exchange or Christmas cookie swap, or being part of a knitting circle are all fun ways to connect with friends old and new. The social support you get from these groups is like a warm hug. Such circles and online communities are the best resources for sourcing raw materials for your projects or in helping you troubleshoot problems.

Save or make money

A hobby sometimes has the potential to expand into a business. After all, what's a better business to get into than something you are passionate about. The pandemic taught us many lessons and one of them is that it doesn't hurt to have alternative revenue streams. A homegrown business as a side hustle is probably the best thing to invest your time in, as a safety net or an added income source. The years 2020–21 have seen a spurt in home chefs making a business out of catering meals from home using app-based delivery services or conducting cooking workshops online. Online workshops for all kinds of crafts and hobbies have a huge market.

Get better at work

Gaetano DiNardi, singer, songwriter and producer from Miami, Florida, writes in a *Harvard Business Review* article, 'Why you should work less and spend more time on hobbies'[3]:

'When I face a tough challenge at work and feel stymied, I can start to question whether I'll ever figure out a successful solution. It's easy to lose creative confidence. But after an hour of shredding on the guitar, hitting notes perfectly, I'm feeling good. I can tell that my brain was craving that kind of satisfaction. And when I face that work project again, I bring the confidence with me.'

Research increasingly supports the fact that involving yourself in creative hobbies when away from work improves performance levels at work. An article on Nature.com explains how a hobby can boost researchers' productivity and creativity.[4] Creative projects are the best way to disconnect from work and

---

[3] DiNardi, G. (7 February 2019). '*Why You Should Work Less and Spend More Time on Hobbies*', Harvard Business Review, https://hbr.org/2019/02/why-you-should-work-less-and-spend-more-time-on-hobbies

[4] Rosen, J. (2018, July 18). '*How a Hobby Can Boost Researchers' Productivity and Creativity*', Nature.com, https://www.nature.com/articles/d41586-018-05449-7

gain some perspective. It's similar to how writers facing writers' block are often advised to step away from their work and do something else, so they can come back to write better. It helps broaden your identity, so 100 per cent of you is not the work you do. Creative hobbies also help avoid burnout.

Now that you are sufficiently convinced as to the numerous benefits of a handmade life, let's see how to make time for creative hobbies.

Making Time to Be a Maker

If you like the idea of making creativity a part of your life, you may find yourself thinking, 'Where am I going to find the time for this?'

Professional work, housework, family time and entertainment are some of the main demands on our time.

The work from home situation makes it tougher to segregate work and life. Having a hard cut-off for work is important. Don't let bits of work linger around you all day. Meetings get scheduled during lunch hours or bedtime. The only way to keep some sanctity of a schedule is to block your calendar for non-negotiable breaks, like a thirty- to forty-five-minute lunchtime where you move away from the screen and enjoy a proper lunch.

I recently read a post on Quora[5] where an Indian woman said that it takes her nine hours a day to cook and feed her family. She was asking the readers if this was normal. It was heartbreaking to read how most of her waking hours were spent slogging in the kitchen, but also heartening to see that she wanted to take steps to reclaim some of those hours for herself. Try to do some time management when it comes to housework such as scheduling certain chores for just once a week instead of daily, menu planning, meal prep, automating daily purchases on apps, shopping just once a week, roping in others to help wherever possible and so on. This can free up a few hours a week.

Spending quality time with the family is non-negotiable. Creative projects make for wholesome non-screen-based family activities. For example, baking or doing upcycling projects with your children, spending time together gardening as a couple, making soaps for each member of the family as a group, as per each person's likes. Almost all projects listed in the book are child-friendly, except for soap making from scratch, which is not suitable for small children and needs extra safety precautions. Then again, melt-and-pour soaps are extremely fun to make with children.

We are aware of how social media and streaming entertainment eat into a bulk of our free time. I open Instagram or Twitter telling myself I'm just going to check them for a minute and, before I know it, an hour has passed. The apps are designed to hold your attention in their steely grip so you can never check in for just a minute. The same goes for any currently trending series on a streaming platform. Steering clear of time sinks will free up many hours of your time. Use reminders on your phone that limit screen time for the apps that you spend the most time on.

Your leisure time is as important as your work time and not to be thrown away mindlessly. Start with one or two things that you truly love or find yourself interested in. Weave some hobby time into weekdays. This will give you small breaks away from work, refresh your mind and add up to significant progress. For example, it's easy to bake sourdough bread on a weekday with little windows of five to ten minutes to attend to the dough. While the entire process takes a minimum of eight hours, it's not something that needs eight hours of your attention.

Whether it's getting back to childhood hobbies or starting something afresh, it can get overwhelming to suddenly start big. Start off with small chunks of hobby time, akin to dipping your toes in water. It is also difficult to cull out one or two hours of continuous free time even on a weekend. Do not get disheartened by that. Even spending twenty minutes on your hobby is an excellent start.

Even though these are hobbies and you are in it for the joy of it, set yourself small goals to help motivate you to finish a project. Finishing a crochet gift before a friend's birthday or sowing seeds in time for a season give you reasons to keep going.

Don't fall for starting trouble. Don't let the pressure to excel at something prevent you from getting started at all. Let me assure you that there is nothing negative about being a dabbler. To engage in arts and crafts, even superficially, is better than to not engage at all. Make sure to avoid unrealistic expectations from yourself and don't focus on being perfect. The key is to just get started.

Be regular with it. My music teachers have instilled in me that thirty minutes of *riyaaz* (practice) every day does much more to make you a better singer than two to three hours of riyaaz once a week. Be it sourdough or soap making, practising a craft regularly makes you excel at it, much more than picking it up randomly once in a while.

The beauty of creativity is in the journey more than the destination. Over the last few years, I had turned into someone who rushed through chores, be it cooking, cleaning or anything else. But, like they say, haste does make waste. Maybe not the final product because of your years of practice and experience, but a waste of the moments that you could well have enjoyed during the process of creating.

Like my music guru, the renowned Indian classical vocalist Shri Mahesh Kale, says, 'Speed should never be your goal. Focus on accuracy and beauty.' When you wipe down the leaves of the houseplants very quickly, it is a stressful chore. If you treat it like a meditative exercise, then wiping each leaf seems to fill up that moment meaningfully and you can take time to admire the shiny green leaves in your home.

There is something about stretching out time, living each moment fully that gives life a gentle and graceful pace. Creative ideas come to you in times of stillness or inspiration from nature or even an image or video you see on social media. Travelling puts you in new surroundings and, if experienced mindfully, makes you imbibe those aesthetics that may inspire you to cook a new dish, try out a new decor style or nudge you to try anything new that you haven't done before.

Triage Your To-Do List

Recently, I listened to a TED talk[6]—'How to manage your stress like an ER doctor' by Darria Long. It was eye-opening in many ways. She talks about how we all tend to say, 'I am crazy busy' and how it is so wrong to keep reinforcing this thought to our own selves.

Triage, or allocating priorities to different tasks, is the best way to go from overwhelmed to calm and collected. It helps you take back control of your time, stress and life.

Here's an example of how to triage your to-do list. If six things need to be done in a day, colour code them in, say, red, orange, green and black. Red for those life-and-death type situations that need attention immediately, orange for necessary but not urgent, green for good to do but not so important, and black for taking it off your plate because you cannot do it. Instantly, you have just one or two things to attend to urgently and not six things that are simultaneously gnawing at you for immediate attention.

---

[6] TED talk by Darria Long https://www.ted.com/talks/darria_long_an_er_doctor_on_how_to_triage_your_busy_life

Fall in Love with the Idea of a Handmade Life

Social media is rife with photos and videos of home-made breads, cakes and coffees from our friends and content creators. If these posts have made you think, 'I wish I could make these too' and then go, 'This is quite tough', 'I don't have the talent/patience to do it' or 'Once was fine, but I don't think I want to do it every day', then this book is just the one for you.

You possibly find making sourdough bread or a bar of soap from scratch intimidating. Reading about the process in detail in this book will take away the fear of the unknown. When the process, requirements and even the opportunity to make a business out of a pursuit are laid out clearly, intimidation leads to inquisitiveness and enthusiasm.

This Handmade Life will show you that it is not at all difficult to make things for everyday use for yourself, your family and friends with only a little time, effort and resources. Eventually, these creative pursuits become a part of life, something that is seamlessly woven into your daily schedule, and are a chance to reap beautiful results. The aim is to indulge in a less consuming, less wanting, more creative and more mindful life.

There is beauty in a slower-paced life in which you take the time to create things that you, your family and your friends will love, and I want to open your eyes to experience this beauty.

This book will show you avenues to spend your leisure time mindfully. It will help you find a creative calling and possibly even earn an income from it. It is the equivalent of attending seven in-depth workshops, all for a very small fee. The reason for this book is to inspire you to get on that creative journey. If the learnings and experiences shared in this book help you enrich your life even a little bit, I will consider it a job well done.

Let's get started!

Sneak Peek at the Chapters

Chapters 1, 2 and 3: Baking and Sourdough, Spices, Fermenting

Some of the projects I write about in this book are merely an extension of what we do every day. Let's take cooking, for example. In India and most parts of the world, the responsibility of cooking skews unfairly towards the women of the house. Cooking also creates many other time-consuming activities on the side, like shopping for ingredients and produce, planning meals around these ingredients, cleaning up after cooking, setting the table, clearing up the table, doing the dishes and the whole cycle starts again. It is a chore rather than something to get all romantic and creative about. I would even go to the extent of saying that it does not leave much time for women to pursue other things that they truly love.

A few people manage to master and convert this everyday household chore into a creative outlet, striking that fine balance between drudgery and creativity, for example, via blogging, photographing, styling, catering, writing and so on. Avenues like baking, bread-making, making fresh spice mixes and fermenting are experiments that kickstart in the kitchen laboratory. Many small-scale businesses in these fields do start off in a passionate cook's kitchen.

Breads, cakes, condiments, spice mixes, lacto-fermented sauces and beverages—all of these are waiting to become a part of your everyday kitchen experiments in the first three chapters.

Chapters 4 and 5: Self-Care

It is a joy and a fulfilling exercise to be able to make your own self-care products, especially for your hair and skin. A home-made soap with your favourite essential oil, natural additions and base oils to suit your skin type makes you look forward to shower time. There are a lot of herbal oils and powders to take care of the hair and skin in a gentle way that also tread lightly on the environment. Both making and using these products are self-care in the truest meaning of the word.

Chapter 6: Gardening

Gardening is another hands-on activity that beautifies the surroundings and nourishes the soul or grows food that nourishes the body. People living in smaller towns with more space in and around the house were always into gardening, be it for aesthetics, keeping the air cool or growing some easy-to-manage vegetables and fruits in a kitchen garden. All over Sikkim, I saw courtyards in front of the houses with neatly laid out gardens. Tall corn plants are often used as a fence around the house. It was such a visual treat to see these kitchen gardens on my long drives around Sikkim. In present times, more and more urban folk are taking to gardening. Indoor plants are a rage for the beauty they bring to the room, making homes greener and more oxygenated. Kitchen gardening or growing your grub is also taking off in urban households, where people make use of a sunny balcony, windowsill or terrace to grow herbs, chillies, tomatoes, lettuce, spinach and more such low space and effort produce. This chapter will help you get your green thumb ready.

Chapter 7: Fabric and Fibre Art

Sewing was an essential craft, like cooking in the earlier days, when ready-made clothes were not the norm. Women of the house would not just repair tears or fix buttons but be able to stitch many of the basic items of clothing. With the gradual shift towards cheap and easily available ready-made garments, the need for stitching exited from our lives. Crochet, knitting and embroidery remain creative pursuits for those who like to keep their hands occupied meaningfully in their free time. I have seen many women go about their knitting or crochet, needles flying at a fast pace while engaging in a busy conversation with the others in the ladies' compartment of Mumbai local trains. This is the Mumbai attitude of not letting a minute be wasted, especially when two- to three-hour train journeys to the city centre are an everyday thing.

Like the popular meme or joke goes, in an Indian home, a new dress will first be worn on occasions, then for general outings, then at home and then the dress becomes a mop or a cleaning cloth. While we can all laugh at this homegrown joke, it is a good lesson in using a piece of fabric to its fullest. Having some tricks up your sleeve helps with effortless upcycling and takes you closer to a zero-waste lifestyle.

Chapter 8: The Business of Handmade

While all these projects are simple, doable and exciting, some of them may catch your fancy more than others. If you ever feel the need to pursue something as a more serious hobby or as a side business, I've got that covered for you. This chapter is like the first friend you have a conversation with about taking your passion project to the next level.

PS: The interviews with experts at the end of each chapter will give you valuable lessons from their journeys and experiences.

Chapter 2

Baking

'It's all about a balancing act between time, temperature and ingredients: That's the art of baking.'
—Peter Reinhart

Growing up in Mumbai, we didn't have an oven at home. In the 1970s and 1980s, ovens were a luxury. It was found only in the kitchens of serious cooking and baking enthusiasts. My aunt, who had a passion for cooking, would sometimes bake a cake in the pressure cooker. I still remember how the eight-year-old me felt, biting into a slice of fresh-out-of-the-cooker warm cake, experiencing joy through food.

It's been nearly twenty years of having an oven at home. There is always the means to bake a cake for no reason at all, but the pressure-cooker cake of my childhood occupies a special, cosy place in my heart.

What is it about flour, sugar and butter coming together in a home-baked cake or cookie that gives unadulterated happiness?

In a study published in the *International Journal of Humanities and Social Science* on the therapeutic effect of cooking as a hobby, researchers concluded that cooking improves a person's well-being. It is also associated with life satisfaction. This could apply to baking more as cooking is an everyday chore while baking still retains some of that special magic.

Precision and Focus

Baking needs precision at every step. Choosing the right ingredients, measuring each one accurately, adding them in the correct order, choosing the right pan, baking at the right temperature and following the correct process for unmoulding, are inherent to the baking process. All these steps bring a sense of having things under control and provide simple things to focus on. Baking needs us to be in the present moment, mindful of the processes that need to be followed, which itself is a way to reduce stress.

Chemistry

Even though all cooking is chemistry, in baking, that chemistry is all the more evident. Consider the transformation of wet dough in just fifteen minutes into the most delectable chocolate chip cookies. Baking provides the instant gratification and joy that we seek, more so in these stressful, unpredictable times of being in the midst of a pandemic. Even in times of normality, baking never fails to deliver a sense of excitement to the humdrum of an everyday routine.

Creativity

Although the recipes need adhering to, there is a lot of scope for creativity when it comes to combining flavours from fresh fruit, nuts and other ingredients like chocolate in different types of bakes.

The creativity involved in the baking process, mindfully putting together all the ingredients and taking the finished product out of the oven—all of these processes contribute to a feeling of contentment.

Baking for others gives us joy. The act of giving a friend something that you have made with your own hands is a very satisfying one, as is knowing that you have made someone's day. Baking for someone is also a way to express your feelings, be it saying thanks or showing empathy or appreciation for people who find it difficult to express this in words, or welcoming a new neighbour.

The Science of Comfort Food

There is a reason why the most common comfort foods are a combination of carbs and fats in some form. When infants cry, they are soothed with milk, whether mother's milk or formula. Milk is carbs and fats combined, and it never fails to soothe babies, making them stop crying or putting them to sleep.

A similar logic may apply in soothing us when we are disturbed or anxious. Most baking is a combination of sugars and fats, initiating the similar primitive response in the brain.

Cakes and bakes made on happy occasions bring forth positive memories and nostalgia, which spell comfort. Research has proven that smells are powerful triggers associated with memory. The aromas of baking can take you back to these happy memories.

Dopamine is one of the feel-good neurotransmitters in the brain. Eating comfort food that you like triggers the dopamine release in the brain, leading to that feel-good sensation. The brain remembers the connection between the food you just ate and the pleasurable after-effects, reinforcing the desire to eat the same food again for that sense of comfort. Even scrolling through Instagram photos of these comfort foods and anticipating them can trigger dopamine release.

Baking through the Pandemic

The COVID-19 pandemic that struck in 2020 has seen a sharp spike in the number of home bakers. People have been making desserts, teacakes and breads at home, sharing them on social media and WhatsApp groups, and inspiring others to do the same. #Quarantinebaking was trending every single day of the various lockdowns around the world. Banana bread had its great resurgence during the pandemic. Baking this simple loaf at home was a coping mechanism. It was a way of finding comfort from creating something delicious out of basic ingredients that the entire family could enjoy.

You just had to mix a bunch of ingredients, put them in the oven and spend a happy forty-five minutes looking forward to the result. It was also a way to reduce food wastage as it made use of the most overripe bananas in the best possible way.

Why bake at home?

1. Even the fanciest of bakes start off using the same few basic ingredients such as flour, sugar, butter and eggs. Bread can be made with just flour, water and salt. There's a reason it is considered the most basic unit of food.

2. Baking is a bonding exercise for the entire family. For someone who is single or lives alone, baking is an exercise in mindfulness and self-care, and it's totally fine to indulge in this pleasurable activity even if it's only for oneself.

3. You can bake at home without using any of the additives and preservatives that are always a part of commercially sold bakes, to ensure a longer shelf life and a stable product. Store-bought bread easily stays good for up to two weeks, and that is not something to be happy about. Commercially available bread has a long list of non-food ingredients that act as preservatives, stabilizers, regulators, etc. Even a not-so-good home-made loaf of bread has more flavour and is closer to the natural form of ingredients than a store-bought loaf of sliced bread.

4. Baking is a good way to get kids interested in cooking as there is a treat waiting at the end of the process. It also makes maths and chemistry interesting for them.

5. At home, it is easier to bake healthier alternatives, such as goodies with reduced fat and sugar, or more nutritious flours, or low glycaemic index (GI) flours for diabetics, etc.

6. There's no better gift for family, friends or neighbours than a home-baked cake or bread.

7. Baking has a positive impact on mental health and mindfulness.

Additives, Preservatives and More

What additives and preservatives are added in mass-produced baked goods?

These could be naturally derived substances or chemicals.

Vinegar, salt and alcohol are some of the natural additives and preservatives. Lecithin, a naturally derived product, is a commonly used stabilizer in cakes and breads.

Acids such as lactic acid, citric acid and tartaric acid are used for their antioxidant and preservative properties. They increase the shelf life of the product by virtue of their antimicrobial function and delaying spoilage.

Caramel is commonly added to white bread to make it look like brown bread, which many people consider to be the healthier option; it is not.

(continued)

Sugar-free bakes make use of sweeteners such as aspartame, sucralose and saccharin.

Although trans fats are banned in packaged brands, they sneak their way into the unbranded baked stuff sold by local bakeries, bakers and small shops. Trans fats or vanaspati give excellent shortening to cookies and biscuits and are much cheaper than using good-quality butter and ghee.

Take a packet of any commercially available bread and you'll see a long list of ingredients, when in reality, all it takes to make bread is flour, water, salt and fat. Substances like bread improvers could be derived from natural sources like soy and corn starch but also chemical agents. Many chemicals are used as dough conditioners, substances that strengthen or improve the texture of the dough. Some of these, such as potassium bromate and azodicarbonamide, are now identified as health safety concerns and are no longer authorized for use in many countries.

Now that we are all set to dive into the beautiful world of baking, let us look at some of the essentials you will need.

An oven is the single most important thing needed for baking.

How to Choose an Oven

The main criteria when it comes to choosing an oven are the type, capacity and price. In today's Indian kitchens, an oven can be either built-in or placed on the countertop.

If you already have a regular microwave oven, then a stand-alone oven-toaster-grill (OTG) is a good place to start. You can get a decent one for Rs 10,000 or so to start with. A mistake most first-time oven buyers make is going for too small a capacity. While it does make sense to start small, it means only very small pans and containers will fit in the oven, and most regular recipes for a standard-sized loaf tin or muffin tray will not work. Gauge your interest and commitment level before deciding on an OTG and go for a minimum of 40 litres capacity. Even if you don't have free counter space, OTGs are quite light as compared to microwaves, and they can be kept on a small table or in another room and brought into the kitchen when you want to bake.

A lot of newbie cooks assume that one can bake in a microwave oven. Please note that the microwave is not suitable for baking anything other than two-minute microwave mug cakes. Baking requires the food to be surrounded by hot air. A microwave directly heats up the molecules of food, which is why the food heats up very rapidly. This method of cooking is not suitable for baking. Most recipes that come up in searches for 'microwave cakes' use the microwave convection oven, which they fail to mention in their titles.

For someone who is setting up their kitchen afresh, a microwave + convection two-in-one oven is a smart buy, which gives you the convenience of switching between two kinds of appliances for the price of one, both cost-wise and counter real estate-wise.

I also see quite a few people unknowingly buying the more expensive two-in-one model when all they want is a microwave to heat food. If you don't have baking on your agenda, then stick to the microwave alone.

The only drawback here is the capacity limitation, which is around 32 litres. It is not possible to bake more than one cake or one tray of cookies at a time. The turntable inside may prevent you from using rectangular baking trays or pans as they may hit the sides as it moves around. The maximum temperature in most microwave-convection ovens is 200°C, while that in OTGs and convection ovens is 240°C. The conditions in microwave-convection ovens may not be the best for bakes like pizzas that need the oven to be preheated to the maximum temperature. These are heavy appliances, not convenient to move around, so they need a fixed place in your kitchen. If you plan to scale up your baking, then it may be a good idea to invest in a separate, larger-capacity OTG.

Built-in ovens are either microwave or convection (electric or gas) ovens. These are definitely a high-commitment investment and not for the occasional dabbler. Gas ovens are helpful if you live in a place with frequent power cuts. After sales service quality needs to be top-notch. Go for these if you plan to regularly bake larger batches or have plans of starting a baking business, be it sales or workshops.

Other Essential Baking Equipment

Now let's take a look at the other things you need for regular baking projects.

Weighing scale: A lot of recipes have ingredients listed in weights and not cups. This is more precise than using metric measurements (cups, spoons). There is also less cleaning up to do as you can use the 'tare' function to bring the weight to zero after adding each ingredient and each can go directly into the bowl.

Measuring cups and spoons: To follow recipes that use metric measurements (cups, spoons), this set is a must-have as you cannot use the regular cups and spoons at home. This will give errors in measurements of ingredients and lead to a failed baking project.

Liquid measuring jug: This is useful for whisking wet ingredients and pouring them into the dry ingredients. Make sure to check the measurements in a jug at eye level.

Silicone spatula: This is possibly the most useful equipment for baking. It is helpful in mixing, smoothing the surface of the batter as well as scraping the batter from the bowls neatly, without leaving a drop behind.

Mixing bowls: We need at least two of these, one for dry ingredients and one for the wet. Another small mixing bowl for whisking one to two eggs is also a useful addition.

Whisk: Metal wire whisks as well as silicone ones work fine. These are useful for whisking eggs, or incorporating air into the dry ingredients, or combining wet ingredients.

Sieve: Different kinds of sieves are available for baking. A sieve helps in combining dry ingredients such as flour, baking powder, cocoa, salt, etc., so that they are well combined, and no lumps of cocoa or baking powder remain. Sieving also incorporates air into the flour.

Zester/microplane: There's nothing quite as refreshing as a lemon loaf with tea. If you, like me, love adding citrus fruits in your bakes, then add this zester or microplane grater to your shopping list. A microplane is a very fine grater that grates the outermost layer of the peel of lemons, limes and oranges. Using a coarser grater sometimes grates the white pith layer under, which has a bitter flavour.

Citrus juicer: You might have one of these at home. A glass juice press in which you can juice any citrus fruits or a lemon squeezer for smaller fruits like lemon and lime is worth buying. A home-made lemon bar is worth its weight in gold, after all.

Hand mixer: To bake basic cakes, you can very well make do with a bowl and a wooden spoon or a whisk. A hand mixer is useful to whip egg whites into stiff peaks, which is a tough task to do by hand, or to combine the wet ingredients well as water and oil tend to not mix easily. Also, an immersion blender is not a substitute for a hand mixer.

Stand mixer: This is definitely a next-level investment. This is a useful implement if you plan to bake larger quantities on a regular basis. Mixing cake batter, cookie dough and bread dough becomes extremely easy with a stand mixer. Do note that it will occupy counter space or space in your cabinets.

Baking Pans and Items for Beginners

(All measurements in inches; material for pans is heavy aluminium unless mentioned otherwise.)

Item	Useful for
1 to 2 circular pans, 8" or 9"	Sponge cakes, birthday cakes, monkey bread, cinnamon rolls
1 square baking tin, 8" or 9"	Brownies, bars, cakes, cinnamon rolls
1 loaf tin (9" × 5" × 3")	Bread loaf, teacakes, pull-apart bread
1 muffin tray, 6 cup or 12 cup	Muffins, cupcakes, frittatas
1 baking tray/cookie tray that fits in your oven	Cookies, pizza, free-form bread, toasting nuts
Wire rack	For cooling unmoulded bakes
Serrated knife	For cutting bread
Cake tester	For checking if the cake is done baking. A skewer or toothpick can also be used.

You've got the information on the oven, pans and other small equipment. Now let's move on to the important items that will ensure that your cakes and bakes come out of the pan neatly without sticking to the bottom.

Baking Pans and Items for Advanced Bakers

Item	Useful for
Cookie cutters in 2 to 3 sizes	Cookies
Springform pan	Cheesecakes
Bundt pans, 6 cup or 12 cup	Pound cakes, teacakes
Ramekins	Chocolate lava cakes, crème brûlée, caramel custard
Pie dish	Pies
Tart pan with removable base	Tarts
Cookie scoops	To get even-sized cookies
Glass pan, 8" square	Savoury bakes like lasagna, cakes, puddings, trifle, caramel custard

Parchment paper or baking paper are your insurance against stuck-in-the-pan cakes. Some of the silent ASMR (Autonomous Sensory Meridian Response) Japanese videos on YouTube take paper folding and lining baking tins to an art form. Leaving some overhang around the sides makes it easy to pull out the steaming hot cakes from the tins. Be careful not to use low-quality tracing paper instead of parchment paper as it can catch fire in the oven. Parchment paper is safe to use up to 250°C without presenting a fire hazard. Aluminium foil is useful to cover up bakes like banana breads midway if you think that the outer surface is getting overly browned well before the batter inside is cooked.

A silicone brush is a nifty implement to make sure the baking tins are uniformly greased with butter or oil. A thin dusting of flour or cocoa powder over this gives you the assurance of a perfect unmoulding in the absence of baking paper.

Build a Baking Pantry

If you would like to bake often, having a dedicated shelf as a baking pantry makes it easy to find all the ingredients for a recipe in one place. Some items like butter, eggs, nuts and dried fruit may have to be refrigerated until you keep them out for an hour or two before getting started with the baking.

Flours—all-purpose flour (maida), wholewheat flour (atta)

Sugars—white sugar, brown sugar, jaggery, honey, date puree, icing sugar

Butter/fats

Baking powder (check best before date)

Baking soda

Yeast—instant yeast

Eggs

Cocoa powder—unsweetened

Chocolate—chips, bars

Vanilla—pods, extract, powder

Nuts—walnuts, cashews, almonds, pistachios

Dried fruit—raisins, dried berries, apricots, dates

Others—almond flour, liqueurs, milk powder, desiccated coconut

Science of Leavening Agents

Baking powder, baking soda and yeast are commonly used leavening agents in baking. All of them release carbon dioxide, which causes cakes and breads to rise. Cakes use either baking powder or soda or a combination of both. It is best not to replace one for the other in a recipe.

Baking soda is sodium bicarbonate. It starts reacting in the presence of an acidic ingredient such as yoghurt, vinegar, lemon juice or buttermilk.

Baking powder is a combination of baking soda and tartaric acid. It starts reacting as soon as it comes into contact with wet ingredients. Double-acting baking powder, as most commercially available brands are, reacts once when the dry and wet ingredients are mixed and then again when the batter is kept in the oven to bake, in the presence of heat.

Baking soda has no expiry date, but baking powder lasts for around a year after the date of manufacturing. Make sure to check the date of manufacturing when you buy baking powder and when using it to bake, especially if you are an occasional baker.

When in doubt, the efficacy of these leaveners can easily be checked. Combine 2 teaspoons of baking powder in ¼ cup of hot water and it should foam vigorously. To check on baking soda's activity, mix 1 teaspoon of baking soda with 2 tablespoons of vinegar and you should see it fizzing. It's best to be sure of the activity of somewhat old leaveners so that the entire lot of ingredients that go into baking a recipe are not wasted due to not-so-active leaveners.

Follow the exact quantity of baking powder and/or soda mentioned in the recipe. Too little of a leavener leads to dense, flat cakes, too much and you get an unpalatable flavour that can put you off cakes.

Yeast is the leavening agent used in breads. These are single-celled fungi, of which hundreds of strains exist. The strain Saccharomyces cerevisiae is mainly used in making bread and brews. Yeast converts sugars into carbon dioxide and alcohol. The gluten in the bread creates a web in which the gases are trapped, giving the bread height and structure.

There are three kinds of yeast available for baking bread in India. Active dried yeast, which is fresh yeast dried into granules, needs proofing (activating) by soaking in lukewarm water and sugar. This is sold under many brands, and looks like cream-coloured homeopathic pills. Most bread-bakers find this to be terribly unpredictable, being more of a miss than hit. So while it's good to know about active dried yeast, it's mainly so that you do not pick it up by accident.

The next variety is fresh yeast, which could either be sold in small packs by your neighbourhood bakery or in half-kilo bricks, which, if you are not running a bakery, is impossible to use before it dies out. This is also avoidable for both new and experienced home bakers.

The last kind and the only kind that I have found to be consistent and reliable is instant yeast. This looks like a coarse powder. As its name suggests, it can be mixed along with the flour and other ingredients and directly kneaded to move into the dough-proving stage. I still like to prove it by mixing with lukewarm water and sugar until I see a fair bit of frothing on the surface, to make sure I don't waste all the other ingredients, just in case the yeast has expired. Instant yeast lasts for nearly a year in the freezer.

The Flours Used for Baking

Most bakers in India use maida and atta, our versions of all-purpose flour and stone-ground wholewheat flour respectively. In the US, UK and Europe, flours with varying strength or protein content are available, depending on what you want to bake.

Cake flour is low in gluten and gives the soft crumb and spongy texture of cake, while bread flour is high in gluten, which is important for the structure of bread. Cake flour is used in delicate cakes like chiffon and angel food cakes.

Self-raising flour is a mix of all-purpose flour, salt and baking powder. It is a convenient product, and no extra baking powder needs to be added to the recipe when self-raising flour is used.

Pastry flour has a slightly higher protein content as compared to cake flour, and is used in delicate cakes, muffins, cookies and pie crust.

Cake flour: 7–8.5 per cent protein
Pastry flour: 8.5–9.5 per cent protein
All-purpose flour: 10–12 per cent protein
Bread flour: 12–13 per cent protein

To get	How to make	
1 cup self-raising flour	1 cup (125 g) maida + 1.5 tsp baking powder + ½ tsp salt	Combine and sift twice
1 cup cake flour	1 cup minus 2 tbsp (114 g) maida + 2 tbsp (16 g of corn flour (corn starch)	Sift two to three times
Pastry flour	1 cup (125 g) maida + ⅓ cup (45 g) cake flour	Sift twice and store
Bread flour	1 cup (125 g) maida + 1 tbsp (9 g) vital wheat gluten	Combine well in a bowl

Resource: Cakesandmore.com /Suma Rowjee

A note on sourdough breads

During the lockdown, the supermarket shelves in many cities abroad first ran out of bread loaves, then flour and then yeast. Faced with a shortage of bread and yeast, people took to sourdough making, which is essentially harnessing the power of the wild yeast around you.

It is fascinating how flour, salt, water and time (and an oven of course) can give birth to the most amazing loaf of bread. A sourdough bread has a tangy flavour that can range from mild to aggressive, a chewy texture and a crackling crust. It can be baked into a variety of shapes and breads such as boules, loaves, baguettes, batards and so on.

True sourdough bread does not make use of yeast for leavening. It uses a live sourdough starter, a fermented culture that acts as a natural leavening agent. The starter can be taken from someone who makes sourdough regularly or can be made from scratch, as is explained in detail in one of the projects below. The starter can be kept fed for decades to give a steady supply of wild yeast to bake breads (and other sourdough dishes) at home. Each time the starter is fed, a portion of it is discarded. Most sourdough bakers hate to throw away the discard, which is rich in live cultures. It can be used to make many other dishes such as dosas, pancakes, khameeri roti, naan, crumpets, waffles, cakes and so on.

We Indians are not new to using wild yeast in our cooking. Idlis, dosas, appams, toddy, all make use of wild yeast. Sourdough starters are a combination of yeast and bacteria. Yeast multiplies in the presence of sugars (flour) and releases carbon dioxide and alcohol. The carbon dioxide is responsible for the bubbles and the alcohol gives the bread its characteristic flavour. The lactic acid bacteria release acids during the process of fermentation, which gives the bread its tangy flavour.

How to Learn Baking

The Internet

The Internet has made it easy to learn basic baking. Be it old-fashioned blogs or Instagram videos or

YouTube, there is a ton of baking content out there. Follow bloggers who are known to test their recipes thoroughly before sharing them, otherwise there is the risk of ingredients and time being wasted. Videos are a good way for beginners to learn some of the basic techniques like measuring ingredients, lining a baking tin, mixing the batter, stretching and folding the dough, shaping bread, etc.

Cookbooks

These are somewhat more reliable than the free content on the Internet as the recipes are always tested. You can have the book at an arm's reach in your kitchen to bake from.

Workshops

In-person, hands-on workshops are the best way to learn a skill like baking. The pandemic has led to a rise in online workshops for nearly every skill, and baking is one of them. While online workshops allow you to see the teacher in action and possibly cook along, you don't get to learn some hands-on techniques like kneading, mixing dough, etc.

Interview with Pooja Dhingra of Le15 India

If you are on social media, Pooja Dhingra needs no introduction. A graduate of hospitality from César Ritz Colleges, Switzerland, and trained at Le Cordon Bleu, Paris, for a Patisserie Diploma, Pooja started the Le15 brand in 2010. She has been featured on the Forbes 30 Under 30 list both in India and Asia.

She is the author of five books and the host of an extremely popular podcast called #NoSugarCoat. Pooja is a huge inspiration for youngsters in India who want to pursue their passion of baking. She lives and works in Mumbai.

Hi Pooja! Do share a recap of your journey for our readers.

I grew up baking. It was always a part of my life, but I never really saw it as a career option. Being a chef then wasn't as cool as it is today. I started off wanting to be a lawyer and I went to law school for two weeks when I was seventeen. It made me realize that I didn't want to be a lawyer. I told my parents that I wanted to get into the food business. They were very supportive about my decision, but they insisted that I get a proper education. I went to Switzerland to pursue my culinary education. Entering the pastry kitchen, I realized this is what I want to do. At twenty-two, I decided to continue my culinary education at Le Cordon Bleu in Paris, where I fell in love with the macaron. And that's how the macaron came to India.

What is your earliest memory of baking?

My mom and aunt were avid bakers, and I was their little kitchen helper. I would come back from school and help my mom make chocolates for her small baking business.

What is your take on people who find their passion in their childhood or teens versus those who stumble upon it much later in life with a full-fledged career going on?

Age or time does not matter as long as you discover what you want to do. It is not necessary to convert every passion into a full-fledged profession. In my class in Le Cordon Bleu, Paris, my closest friend was a fifty-five-year-old Chinese American whose life's mission was to make the perfect croissant. There are many things that I am passionate about, for example, screenplay writing or teaching yoga, but I may not end up pursuing them full time. As long as you find that spark within you and you follow that spark, you will find the right path.

What are the absolute basics a newbie baker should have to get started with baking?

The best thing about baking is that it is a low-risk and low-demand activity to bake from home. Other than a good oven, all you need are some basics like bowls, spatula and whisk, and you are good to start. When I got back from Paris, I used to experiment in my parents' home kitchen all the time.

In baking, it's always said to follow the recipe to a T, unlike in cooking. Do you believe that someone who's just getting started should strictly follow this, or is it okay to play with your instincts sometimes and wander away from a recipe?

Always follow the recipe, measure the ingredients. Baking is so precise and scientific, if someone has said 100 g of butter in a recipe, there is a reason for it. Brownies and cookies are a bit forgiving, unlike some of the exacting French desserts like macarons and choux pastry where even 5 g of excess liquid or dry ingredients can result in a failed recipe. Recipes like these need absolute precision. Experiment with flavours, not with measurements or main ingredients.

What would you recommend as the first few bakes for a beginner?

The first thing I made was a brownie. Brownies are a good place to start, because they are always delicious.

I also love cookies, because I find them warm and comforting. Eventually you'll get the hang of how different batters and doughs work and you can keep adding on from there to get into basic cakes. Cookies and brownies are a good place to start for a newbie baker.

We mostly equate baking with sweet treats, especially in India, even though in our own culture we have a huge repertoire of savoury snacks. What are some of the savoury bakes a home baker should learn and make?

In Mumbai, the Irani bakery culture has its puffs and khari biscuits, which are complex to make at home. Savoury quiches and cookies are good to make at home.

Custards and tarts need eggs, and in India, many people like baking without eggs.

When a hobby becomes a full-time profession, does it lose some of the initial joy and excitement?

The start of the pandemic did throw such questions at me. Being on autopilot for so many years, running a business with 100 employees, it becomes overwhelmingly about everything other than being in the kitchen. No matter what your passion is, when it becomes your full-time job, you need to keep asking yourself why you're doing this, because it does get diluted over time. Coming back to the original why is very important to keep reminding yourself. That's how my next book *Coming Home* came about. I enter the kitchen every day, and I remind myself how much I love baking.

The pandemic saw the rise of a number of home chefs and bakers. If someone wants to transition from a hobby to a small business, what are some of the tips you have to offer them?

Testing the market is the most important thing, which happens when you start selling to people other than friends and family.

It all depends on what your goal is at the end of the day. The next steps need to be taken accordingly. If you want to keep it very small, that's perfectly fine.

Finding a space, setting SOPs (standard operating procedures), government regulations and licences, hiring people are all some of the initial requirements if you are planning to scale up the home-baking business. Set a goal first and then work backwards.

How can a small baking business leverage social media for sales?

When I got on social media, I found it a way of storytelling and communicating what I was going through at each time. One size never fits all. For food, Instagram seems to be the best platform as of now. Identify your niche and what you bring to the table that no one else does. Each one of us has that one thing that no one has, find that and work on it.

What really helped me was authenticity. Be who you are. The minute people see that, they appreciate it. The other thing is to be consistent. Decide the medium that works for you and consistently follow through. It takes a while to see the shift and build a strong community. Look at it as a platform to showcase yourself and your work. Target people in your area to start with.

What is your go-to bake to destress?

I would say anything with chocolate. I made a lot of cookies in lockdown because I find them comforting. I have a special connection with macarons. I find it to be a meditative process, and it clears your head.

What is your favourite ingredient?

It is chocolate. My friend in culinary school tells me that my face changes when I'm with chocolate. Other than chocolate, it would be vanilla. Vanilla bean elevates everything.

Sweet or savoury?

Do I even need to answer that? *laughs*

Interview with Anita Tikoo of *A Mad Tea Party* on Sourdough Baking

Anita Tikoo has a bachelor's in architecture from the School of Planning and Architecture (SPA), Delhi, and a master's in landscape architecture from Kansas State University, USA. She was an adjunct/visiting professor at SPA, Delhi, between 2000 and 2018.

Anita is a practising landscape architect who enjoys cooking with seasonal ingredients. In her terrace garden she grows some of the foods that fuel the ferments in her Delhi kitchen. She has presented her work at many national and international fermentation festivals and symposia. She conducts food workshops (presently online) where like-minded people join her in the kitchen on weekends to cook with locally sourced seasonal ingredients. She has been baking sourdough breads at home for years using her lively wild yeast starter and local flours. Anita blogs about food matters at *A Mad Tea Party* (https://madteaparty.wordpress. com/) and the Instagram handle is @a_madteaparty

How did you get bitten by the sourdough bug?

In 2010, I made my first sourdough starter and sourdough bread using the starter. There wasn't much interest in those times around sourdough baking. I wrote about it in detail on my blog but didn't get too much feedback from my readers on this thing I was all excited about. There wasn't much information available online nor was there any access to books to take it to the next level. So, after one year, I finished off the starter in a batch of pancakes and there was a lull for five years.

Five years later, Pamela Timms, food writer and author, moved back from New Delhi to the UK and on reaching home she posted a picture of a sourdough starter she was making, on her Instagram feed. That made me want to do it all over again in the peak of Delhi summer and then there was no looking back.

How has your journey been, and do you have anything to say to inspire a newbie sourdough baker?

Sourdough is as simple or as complex as you would like it to be. You can either skim the surface or plunge into the depths. It's fine to start off knowing a little bit about it. Too much science sometimes comes in the way of doing something. It may feel overwhelming and intimidating. Given that most Indians deal with fermented dough and dahi on a daily basis without getting into the science of it, sourdough is also doable in a similar fashion. Fermentation that relies on wild yeast and bacteria is all there is to sourdough. We need to be more intuitive about it. Start out simple. Do not plunge straight away into wholegrain breads. Make simple recipes like pancakes to start with. The first step is just to take care of the starter. Familiarize yourself with that process, and then you can get into baking.

On my journey, I didn't follow too many rules, and I hadn't done too much research. Even then, I felt like my sourdough breads were always very good. I started reading more about it only after a year of regular baking.

Yeasted bread versus sourdough—what are your thoughts?

Don't judge your bread, whether you are making it from yeast or sourdough. Given that making your bread is already complex, don't complicate it further by making wholegrain recipes at the start or trying to use sourdough for your first-ever loaf of bread. It's like directly jumping from grade one to five. Start with a basic white bread, then add up to 20 per cent atta and so on. In the early days, don't be in a rush. Sourdough is not about hurrying. It's a lesson in patience.

What are the basic things that are required in terms of ingredients and equipment?

A good oven is a must for sure. A bench scraper because sourdough is a bit stickier than regular doughs. A kitchen scale. Besides that, you don't need too much.

I had once baked a lovely sourdough loaf with the starter I had carried along to a friend's home in a tea plantation in Siliguri with a very basic oven and almost nothing else.

Do you believe in weighing all the ingredients or can we follow our instincts?

There are different approaches in sourdough. I believe in weighing ingredients.

The things we do without measuring, like in idlis, we still measure volumes and ratios. While making idli–dosa batter, the quantity is also large so if you are off by a bit it is not going to matter. If you are making a small loaf of say 200 g, and you are off by 10 g of water, it's 5 per cent extra water, which makes a big difference. It will impact how the dough is going to behave. A wetter dough ferments at a different rate. Temperature is also an everyday variable, we don't have a control on that variable. A professional set-up has a proofer to control the temperature.

A beginner does not have familiarity with the process. Maybe after twenty years, I can eyeball the ingredients, but it's not like chapati dough that we make every day. For a beginner, weighing ingredients is essential so that you have as many things constant as possible to make it easier. Bread gets better with time as your skills and judgement are improving. I practically bake the same loaf as I am still learning the intricacies of this recipe. If I change a recipe every time I make a sourdough, I will not understand why my bread turned out a certain way. So, definitely, use the kitchen scales.

We end up pursuing different hobbies. Does it get boring after a few years? What makes you stick around and keeps you excited?

The complexity of sourdough keeps you interested. You're never done learning it. Even with the same recipe, breads turn out different each time. Change a flour brand or an added flour to the blend, and you get a totally new result. I'm still nowhere near the ending.

It is as exciting to me today as it was five years ago. Each time I open the lid of the Dutch oven to see the baked bread, I am as excited.

What are a couple of tips for newbie sourdough bakers?

Give yourself time to become familiar with your starter. Don't rush into baking a loaf of bread. Feed your starter, see how it is responding.

Have one classic recipe and for three to six months just practise the same thing a couple of times a week. There's only so much you can learn by watching or learning. You can become a good baker only with practice. The recipes are simple, but it's about the focus, paying attention to the details. Don't judge your bread and don't look for instant results.

Any advice for people who want to take up sourdough baking as a business?

There is a longer cycle of production in sourdough as compared to regular breads. Starting early in the morning, the loaves will be ready late in the evening. So space becomes an important requirement for proving.

Baking also takes longer; the minimum bake time is around forty-five minutes.

Bulk fermentation needs to be maintained at a certain temperature, so that is an investment.

People have to be willing to pay a premium for sourdough bread.

Other than selling bread, other things that can be done in this space are sourdough crackers that are quick and don't require as much space, other forms of fermentation, teaching workshops, etc.

What are your top three sourdough dishes?

- Sourdough crackers are a complete people pleaser and my absolute favourite.
- Focaccia because it is very forgiving, gives you a great bread without any effort.
- Pancakes with rice flour and sourdough.

Projects

These are some basic recipes in baking and sourdough that are useful for everyday consumption, special occasions or gifting to friends.

Once you have mastered the basic recipes, you can play around with different flavours in the cakes, muffins and breads to create your own versions.

1. Easy One-Bowl Chocolate Cake   56
2. Chocolate Chip Cookies   58
3. Tea-Time Cake   60
4. ABC Breakfast Muffins   61
5. One Hell of a Healthy Cake   63
6. Basic Loaf of Bread (with instant yeast)   66
7. Sourdough Starter   69
8. Sourdough Waffles   74
9. Rustic Sourdough Bread   75

1. Easy One-Bowl Chocolate Cake

The pandemic lockdowns taught us that we all need to know how to bake a basic birthday cake or just a cake to make an ordinary day special. It is a true life skill, because we cannot let birthdays go by without a nice cake to celebrate. This cake can be made with the usual pantry ingredients.

Serves 6-8.

Gather

1 cup (125 g) all-purpose flour (maida)
½ cup + 2 tbsp (125 g) granulated sugar (run it in the mixer to get fine granules)
⅓ cup (~40 g) cocoa powder
¾ tsp baking powder
½ tsp baking soda
1 egg (see egg replacement tip in the notes)
½ cup (~120 ml) milk (use plant-based milk to make it vegan)
¼ cup (60 ml) vegetable oil
1 tsp vanilla extract
Up to ½ cup (~120 ml) boiling water

Chocolate ganache icing
~ ½ cup (100 g) chopped milk or dark chocolate bar
½ cup (~100 ml) high fat cream

Make

Preheat the oven at 180°C.

Grease and line the bottom of an 8" round cake tin with parchment paper.

Combine all the ingredients in a large bowl except the boiling water. Mix with a wooden spoon until well combined.

Add the boiling water to this mixture little by little with repeated stirring. The batter will get considerably thin and pourable. Don't add more water at this stage.

Scrape this batter into the greased and lined cake tin. Push some of the batter from the centre to the sides so that it is a little indented in the centre. This will ensure your cake rises uniformly and does not dome up in the centre.

Place in the centre rack of the oven and bake for around twenty-five to thirty-five minutes. After twenty-five minutes, remove the tin and insert a skewer/dry spaghetti into the cake to see if it comes out clean. If not, bake for another five to ten minutes until the cake is thoroughly baked.

Remove from the oven, cool for ten to fifteen minutes. Remove from the tin carefully and cool on a wire rack thoroughly before slicing.

To prepare the ganache, chop the chocolate bar into small pieces. Heat the cream in a small saucepan. Once the cream is hot, add the chopped chocolate to the cream and keep stirring until it is completely melted and you get a glossy ganache.

You can pour hot ganache over the cooled cake so it drips down the sides for a nice effect. Else, let the ganache cool in the fridge for fifteen minutes until it is thick and spreadable. Spread this over the cake with a palette knife and top with sprinkles or edible decorations of choice.

Note: For the eggless version, in a small bowl combine 1 tbsp ground flaxseed with 3 tbsp hot water and whisk until thick and gelatinous. Use this instead of the egg.

2. Chocolate Chip Cookies

You find good recipes in the unlikeliest of places. There was a time my son was addicted to the Geronimo Stilton series of books. Now, you'd find a few surprise recipes scattered in these books. My son found a chocolate chip cookie recipe in one of these books and he would not rest until we tried it out. Those were probably the best chocolate chip cookies we've made. This recipe is adapted from the Geronimo surprise recipe.

Serves 6–8.

Gather

1-¼ cup (150 g) all-purpose flour (maida)
½ tsp baking soda
½ tsp salt
½ cup (113 g) soft butter (at room temp., use a 100 g pack + 2 tsp)
⅓ cup (65 g) granulated sugar (run it in the mixer to get fine granules)
⅓ cup (65 g) brown sugar light (or powdered jaggery)

1 egg (check notes for egg replacement)
1 tsp vanilla extract
1 cup (170 g) chocolate chips (or a chopped bar)

Make

Sieve the flour, baking soda and salt. Keep aside.

In a bowl, place the butter and sugars. With a wooden spoon or an electric beater, beat the butter and sugar until pale and creamy.

Add the egg and beat until well incorporated.

Add the vanilla extract and mix well.

To this, add the dry ingredients and mix until well combined.

Add the chocolate chips and gently mix until uniformly distributed.

Cover the bowl well and refrigerate for at least an hour or even overnight.

Preheat the oven to 180°C.

Scoop out a tablespoon worth of dough for each cookie on the tray, keeping an inch space between the cookies to allow for expansion.

Bake for approximately ten minutes. Remove and allow to cool on a wire rack for ten minutes during which time the cookies will harden further. Place in an airtight container.

Note: To replace the egg, in a small bowl combine 1 tbsp ground flaxseed with 3 tbsp hot water and whisk until thick and gelatinous. Use this instead of the egg.

3. Tea-Time Cake

I love plain and simple teacakes over any of the cakes smothered with cream, frosting or, even worse, fondant. While you can make teacakes flavoured with any seasonal fruit, dried fruit, fruit infusions or teas or even coffee, this basic, middle-sweet one flavoured with vanilla or sometimes desified with powdered green cardamom is truly my favourite.

Serves 6–8.

Gather

1-¼ cups (150 g) all-purpose flour
1 tsp baking powder
¼ tsp baking soda
¾ cup (150 g) sugar (finely ground)
¼ cup (60 ml) rice bran oil (or any neutral oil)
3 eggs
¼ cup (60 ml) full cream milk
1 tsp vanilla extract
¼ cup (40 g) chopped cashews (optional)

Make

Preheat the oven at 180°C.

Grease and line the bottom of a 7–8" round cake tin with parchment paper.

Sieve the flour, baking powder and baking soda.

In another bowl, whisk the sugar and oil until creamy. You can use an electric whisk for this purpose.

Add in eggs, milk and vanilla extract and whisk for one or two minutes until light and airy.

Add the dry ingredients in three batches, stirring lightly after each addition until well incorporated.

Scrape out the batter into the lined tin.

Top with chopped cashew nuts if using.

Bake at 180°C for twenty-five to thirty-five minutes until a skewer comes out clean. Remove from the oven and cool for fifteen minutes before unmoulding the cake.

Cool for an hour before slicing it. Serve warm.

4. ABC Breakfast Muffins (Apple, Banana, Carrot)

A good breakfast muffin must have a hearty dose of fruits, vegetables and fibre. Do note that these are not cupcakes, so we are deliberately keeping them low on sugar. It is the kind of thing you can grab and go for a snack or a quick healthy bite on the move.

Makes 12 muffins.

Gather

1 cup (120 g) wholewheat flour
½ cup (60 g) buckwheat flour
½ cup (65 g) all-purpose flour
1-½ tsp baking powder
½ tsp baking soda
½ tsp salt
2 tsp ground cinnamon
¼ cup (60 ml) cold pressed sunflower oil
½ cup (100 g) raw cane sugar

2 eggs
1 large apple, grated
2 overripe medium-sized bananas, mashed
1 cup grated carrot (loosely packed)
¼ cup (30 g) mixed seeds (chia, sunflower, pumpkin)
¼ cup (30 g) chopped nuts (any one or a mix)

Make

Preheat the oven at 200°C. Take a 12-cup muffin tray and line each cup with a paper liner.

In a large bowl, pass the dry ingredients (flours, baking powder, baking soda, salt, cinnamon) through a sieve.

In another large bowl, combine the oil, sugar and eggs. Beat using an electric whisk for one to two minutes until the sugar has dissolved and the mixture is fluffy.

Add the carrot, apple and banana and beat for another minute.

Add the dry ingredients to the wet mixture and combine gently using a spatula until no large dry clumps of flour remain. Mix in the nuts and seeds. The muffin batter is ready.

For beautiful domed muffin tops, fill the muffin batter nearly up to the top of each cup. Tap the filled tray a couple of times on the counter to remove any air bubbles.

Place the tray in the preheated oven. After five to seven minutes of baking, reduce the temperature to 180°C and continue baking for another twelve to fifteen minutes. Check by poking a couple of muffins with a tester or skewer to see if they come out clean.

Serve immediately or refrigerate in a box once cooled.

Notes: The same batter can be used to make delicious pancakes or waffles.

You can replace half the grated carrots with grated beets for a serving of another vegetable and a pop of colour.

5. One Hell of a Healthy Cake

What makes a cake healthy? Using a healthier flour option with more nutrition and fibre than all-purpose flour, or a gluten-free flour if that's your version of healthier. Cutting down on refined sugar is also a way of making a cake healthier. Adding nutrient-rich seasonal or dried fruits and nuts also give a cake a healthy boost. Why would one want to make a cake healthy, you may ask. It's nice to indulge a health-conscious family member or friend with this treat or someone who is off refined foods but still wants to enjoy a slice of cake. Do note that jaggery is similar to sugar when it comes to increasing blood glucose levels. Eat this in moderation if you are watching your sugar intake, even though it is a healthy cake.

Serves 8–10.

Gather

9" × 5" loaf tin
1 large apple

1 cup (140 g) ragi flour
1 cup (120 g) wholewheat flour
1-½ tsp baking powder
½ tsp baking soda
3 tbsp (18 g) cocoa powder
½ tsp salt
½ cup (120 g) powdered organic jaggery
2 eggs
½ cup (120 ml) virgin coconut oil*
1 tsp vanilla extract
1 tsp natural vinegar**
½ cup (60 g) chopped walnuts

Make

Prepare the loaf tin by brushing oil on all sides. Cut a parchment paper and place it at the bottom with a sufficient overhang on both the long ends of the pan. Brush the parchment with oil once again.

Preheat the oven at 180°C.

Cut the apple into quarters. Slice the core and seeds and discard. Keep the apple pieces in a small pressure cooker with ½ cup water. Let it come to full pressure on a high flame (one whistle) and then turn off the heat. Once the pressure drops, open the cooker

---

* Most virgin coconut oil has no coconut flavour, but if it does, you can use an extra teaspoon of vanilla extract to mask it.
** Natural vinegar is one with the 'mother'. It could be home-made (check Mango Vinegar recipe on page 159 from the 'Get Fizzy' section), or store-bought. If you don't have natural vinegar, use the same quantity of lime juice.

and remove the cooked apples to a bowl. Tug off the skins and mash the cooked flesh to get applesauce. Measure out ¾ of a cup of the prepared applesauce and keep aside.

Meanwhile, in a pan, dry roast the ragi flour over a low flame for four to five minutes. Do not brown the flour. This is to reduce some of the characteristic millet aroma in the flour.

In a large bowl, pass the dry ingredients (ragi flour, wheat flour, baking powder, baking soda, salt, cacao powder) through a sieve.

In another large bowl, combine the apple sauce, jaggery, eggs, coconut oil and vanilla using an electric whisk for one to two minutes until the jaggery has melted and eggs are fluffy.

Divide the dry ingredients into three batches and add them one part at a time to the wet ingredients, combining gently with a spatula. As one batch is mixed into the wet ingredients, add the second batch and then the third. This is to ensure that you are not over-mixing the batter. Stir in the vinegar and chopped walnuts in the final mixing stage.

Scrape out the batter into the prepared loaf tin and tap it on the counter a couple of times to level it out.

Transfer to the pre-heated oven and bake for forty to forty-five minutes. A tester or a skewer should come out clean when poked into the centre of the loaf.

Remove the tin and allow it to cool for five to ten minutes. Run a knife along the short ends of the loaf and using the overhanging parchment, lift out the cake.

Place on a wire rack and cool for at least thirty minutes before slicing it.

6. Basic Loaf of Bread (with instant yeast)

This part wholewheat bread is as basic as it gets—a no-fail recipe that gets you a good loaf of bread every single time. Bake it at night and you'll be able to slice it neatly for breakfast. A home-baked loaf of bread is also perfect to cut into thick slices for French toast.

Gather

9" × 5" loaf tin
1 cup (240 ml) lukewarm water (you should be able to dip your little finger in the water to a count of 10 without any discomfort)
2 tsp sugar
1-¼ tsp instant yeast
1 cup (120 g) wholewheat flour
1-½ tsp salt
2 tbsp (30 ml) oil (olive or sunflower)
2 cups (250 g) all-purpose flour

Make

MIXING

In a large bowl, combine lukewarm water, sugar, yeast and wholewheat flour using a wooden spoon. It's all right if there are a few lumps of flour. Cover the bowl with a clean towel and keep aside for ten to fifteen minutes until it is bubbly on the surface.

Now stir in the salt and oil. Mix in all-purpose flour one cup at a time using the wooden spoon. When the dough cannot be mixed with the spoon any more, plop it on a clean, floured surface.

KNEADING

Knead the dough, adding a few tablespoons of water to bring it together. Coat your hands and the work surface with just enough flour to prevent the dough from sticking. Knead for five minutes, turning the dough by a quarter of a circle each time, so that the entire dough gets kneaded well. At the end of this kneading session, when you lightly press the dough with your fingertips, it should bounce right back. Make a rough ball of the dough.

PROVING

Oil the mixing bowl well and put the dough into the bowl. Cover with the towel or a loose-fitting lid. Keep the bowl in a warm place for the dough to prove.

Proving is the process of the dough doubling in size due to the yeast reacting with sugars to produce carbon dioxide. This should take 1 to 2 hours, depending on your room temperature.

SHAPING

Transfer the proven dough on to a floured surface and spread out into a rectangle with roughly the width corresponding to the length of your loaf tin.

To shape the loaf, the width of the rectangle should be towards you. Fold the lower third of the dough upwards towards the middle. Now fold the right and left sides towards the centre with some overlap. The dough will now resemble an open envelope. Take the top free side and stretch and fold it downwards.

Line a 9" × 5" loaf tin with baking paper.

Gently pick up the shaped dough and transfer it seam side down in the lined loaf tin. If you don't have a loaf tin, then place the shaped dough on a baking tray. The end result will be more free form with less height than the one baked in the loaf tin.

SECOND PROVING

Cover the loaf tin with a floured cotton towel and let it rise for thirty minutes. It should come slightly above the rim of the loaf tin, if you are baking a loaf.

BAKING

Preheat the oven to 190°C.

Carefully remove the towel and slash the top of the loaf with a sharp knife. Bake for about thirty minutes until the crust is golden brown and the loaf sounds hollow when tapped on the bottom.

RESTING AND SLICING

Cool the bread on a rack. Slice when cooled.

Using the same dough, you can make other goodies like grissini and focaccia.

Grissini/Breadsticks: Roll any leftover dough into long ropes, sprinkle some coarse salt and bake at 180°C for twenty to thirty minutes, turning the baking tray once midway. Serve with soups or a dip.

Focaccia: Use half the recipe for the basic bread loaf. Prep a rimmed baking tray by brushing with oil. Line with parchment or aluminium foil.

After the first proving, when the dough has doubled, stretch and press dough into the prepared baking tray. Make dents using fingertips all around the dough. Drizzle a good quantity of olive oil. Press sprigs of rosemary, cherry tomatoes or sliced onions in the dents. Preheat oven to 250°C. Sprinkle coarse salt and bake the focaccia until golden brown, around fifteen minutes. Let cool to room temperature before cutting into squares.

7. Sourdough Starter

An active sourdough starter in the fridge is your go-to supply of wild yeast to bake a beautiful, aromatic loaf of bread, with nothing more than flour and salt.

You can get access to a starter from a neighbour or friend who bakes sourdough bread, a sourdough bakery who may sell it to you or gift it to you if you are a regular customer. If you don't have access to any of these then your option is to make one from scratch, which is not bad at all. All you need is flour, honey and water and a few minutes of effort over eight to ten days, after which you have a starter pet in your kitchen that you can christen and feed regularly.

A sourdough starter can be made with many other foods like soaked legumes and grains, which kick-starts fermentation in idli batter. But using flour is a more systematic and predictable approach for a beginner.

You will also get some quantity of sourdough discarded every day, which is a great starting point for many breakfasts as you will see in the following recipes.

Many recipes ask for the flour and water to be weighed precisely in grams. This is an easy method and you can use basic measuring cups.

Gather

A 2-cup size transparent glass jar/bowl/mug
Atta or wholewheat flour
Maida or all-purpose flour for the feeds
2 tsp honey (or 1 tsp organic jaggery)
Small silicone spatula (helps to clean the sides of the jar well)

Make

DAY 1

Weigh a clean dry glass jar (minus lid) and make a note of the weight of the jar. You can either write this with a permanent marker on the jar or use a label to stick on the jar. This will be useful later in the process.

8 a.m.:

Mix ½ cup of wholewheat flour (atta) and ½ cup water in a jar along with 2 tsp honey (or crushed jaggery) until well combined. Scrape down the sides. Cover with a dish or a loose-fitting lid.

After each feed, securing a rubber band at the level of the starter on the outside of the bottle or drawing a line with a marker pen helps understand how much the starter has risen.

8 p.m.:

Stir well, scrape down sides and cover with the dish or loose lid. (Initially, the starter needs attending to roughly every twelve hours.)

DAY 2

If you live in a hot place, you may see bubbles on the surface just twenty-four hours after mixing flour and water in which case you can start the discarding-feeding cycle on day 2 itself.

If you don't see any activity, just stir the mixture twice in the day twelve hours apart, similar to day 1.

DAY 3

If the starter looks active with bubbles on the surface, you can start the discarding and feeding cycle. Feeding in sourdough parlance is to give the starter a fresh dose of flour and water which is used as food by the bacteria and yeast.

Feeding is with all-purpose flour or maida. Discard half the contents of the jar.*

To the remaining contents in the jar, add ¼ cup maida and ¼ cup water. Stir very well, scrape the sides using the silicone spatula and cover loosely with a lid or a dish. Let this rest for twenty-four hours.

After the feed, the starter will rise. This happens due to the carbon dioxide released by the yeast that multiplies after being fed sugars. Once all of the feed has been consumed, the level of the starter will fall back towards the original level marked with a rubber band or market. This is the time for the next feed.

DAYS 4, 5, 6

Discard half the contents of the jar. To the remaining contents in the jar, add ¼ cup maida and ¼ cup water. Stir very well, scrape the sides and cover loosely with a lid or a dish. Do this every twelve hours, for example, 8 a.m. and 8 p.m.

This process should continue until the starter seems to double in volume in four to six hours. You can tell this by checking the initial level marked with a rubber band or marker. This process takes around six to ten days or more depending on the weather where you live.

What we are looking for is a starter that rises and falls at predictable rates. The surface should have a

---

* If you don't want to throw away the discard, you can keep collecting this in a separate jar in the fridge labelled 'discard'. Use the discard in recipes like waffles (page 74) or dosas.

mix of large and small bubbles and will be risen. This is your sourdough starter, also called 'mother'.

Maintaining the sourdough starter

The ready sourdough starter can now be refrigerated or used to make a levain, which is the starting point for any sourdough bread.

The refrigerated sourdough starter should be ideally refreshed (fed) every week to ten days. Refrigeration slows down the activity of bacteria and yeast so they don't need as much food as they would at room temperature. Those who bake sourdough bread or other recipes every day can leave the starter at room temperature and feed it every day. For the more casual baker who is likely to bake once a week, feeding the starter once a week and using the discard to bake bread is a more practical option.

To refresh the starter, one way to do it is to leave 25 g of starter in the bottle (this is why it is good to know the weight of the empty bottle beforehand) and feed with 100 g of water and maida each. Stir thoroughly. Cover and keep at room temperature for one to two hours until it starts showing bubbling activity, after which you can refrigerate it.

To make levain

Take 25 g from the mother starter and combine with 50 g each of maida and water. This will take four to six hours to be ready to use along with flour and water to make sourdough bread.

Some factors that affect the time taken for the levain to be ready to use:

Fermentation is faster with atta or multigrain flour and slightly slower with maida.

The quantity of starter used—more the quantity of starter used, faster the fermentation.

The ambient temperature—the higher the temperature, the faster the fermentation.

8. Sourdough Waffles

The good thing about making a sourdough starter is that you have a live culture to use up in a variety of dishes on each of the eight to ten days that you are feeding the starter. This can also be made using the discard obtained when you do the weekly feed for your mature starter.

Gather

½ cup (140 g) sourdough starter
¾ cup (94 g) all-purpose flour/maida
1 cup (130 g) wholewheat flour/atta
1-¾ cup (420 ml) buttermilk*
½ tsp baking soda
1 tsp salt
2–3 tbsp (25–38 g) sugar
¼ cup (60 ml) melted butter
2 eggs

---

* This can either be cultured buttermilk that you get by churning butter from cream or use thinned out home-made yoghurt. The sourdough starter will provide enough tanginess to the waffles so do not use sour yoghurt or buttermilk.

Make

In a large bowl, combine the sourdough starter, maida, atta and half the buttermilk using a whisk. Keep this covered for one hour. Add the remaining buttermilk, baking soda, salt, sugar, melted butter and whisked eggs. Gently combine to make a smooth batter.

Cover and keep aside for ten minutes.

Preheat a waffle iron. Brush both surfaces with oil or use a non-stick spray. Ladle the recommended quantity of batter as per the size of your waffle maker. Close the top and cook until the waffle is golden brown and crisp on both sides. Serve immediately or keep the waffles warm in an oven preheated at 120°C until ready to serve.

9. Rustic Sourdough Bread

Now that you have an active sourdough starter and the knowledge to make a levain, it's time to get baking. By percentage, a good measure of levain to bake a sourdough is 20 per cent of the weight of the flour, or 1 cup levain for 5 cups flour if you go by metric measurements.

You don't need any special equipment like a stand mixer, but you do need an oven that goes up to 240°C to 250°C and, ideally, a heavy cast iron pot (Dutch oven) with an oven proof lid. A heavy-duty baking tray covered with a thick parchment paper or silicone mat can be used instead.

Makes 1 large or 2 small loaves.

Gather

~¾ cup (100 g) atta
3-¼ cups (400 g) maida
2 tsp (10 g) salt
⅓ cup (100 g) levain (from the sourdough starter recipe on page 69)
Little less than 1-½ cups (350 g) water

Make

In a large bowl, mix atta, maida and salt with a whisk until well combined.

In another large bowl, whisk the levain into the water.

AUTOLYSE

Add the dry flours into the water. Using a silicone spatula or a wooden spoon, mix all the ingredients together until no large dry spots of flour remain. Sprinkle up to an extra 1 tbsp of water if the dough is too dry. Cover with a cloth or a lid and let this sit for forty-five minutes. This is called the 'autolyse' phase.

BULK RISE (WITH OR WITHOUT STRETCH AND FOLD)

Knead the dough into a ball. Cover and let it rise until doubled in volume. This could take three to six hours depending on how potent the starter is and the ambient temperature.

Optionally, you could add the 'stretch and fold' steps during the bulk rise phase. This technique is said to give the bread good structure and height and also trap some of the gases within the dough.

To do this, after thirty minutes of bulk rise, perform one set of stretch and fold. Wet your fingers by dipping them in water so that the dough does not stick. Pick up one corner of the dough, stretch it gently and fold it over on the opposite side. Rotate the bowl by 180 degrees and repeat the same process. This process done once for each of the four corners of the dough (east, west, north and south) makes one set of stretch and fold. You can do this process in the bowl itself or on a floured countertop.

Keep the bowl covered with a cloth between each of the stretch and fold sets. If the dough is on the counter, then cover it with a bowl.

Repeat the set after thirty minutes. You can do this process three to four times, which will take a total of ninety minutes to two hours. (Watch YouTube videos given in the resources to understand the stretch and fold techniques better.)

SHAPE

Once the dough has doubled in volume, divide it into two halves for two smaller loaves or keep it whole for a larger loaf.

Shape it into a boule (round) or any other preferred shape, keeping the seam sides down. (Watch YouTube videos given in the resources to understand the different ways to shape a dough.)

SECOND RISE

Transfer the shaped dough to a parchment-lined Dutch oven or a lined heavy baking tray. Keep covered with the lid or a flour-dusted cotton towel (in case of baking tray) and allow for the dough to rise for thirty minutes to an hour. It need not double in size during this rise.

BAKING

Preheat the oven between 220–250°C for fifteen minutes towards the end of the second rise period. Score the dough with a sharp serrated knife or blade either in the centre or make two or three diagonal lines. Transfer the baking tray or the Dutch oven into the preheated oven. If using a tray, add some ice cubes to the bottom of the oven to generate steam for a good rise to the bread.

Reduce the oven temperature to 200°C. Bake with the lid on for twenty minutes and then with the lid off for another twenty-five minutes until the crust is a deep golden brown in colour.

RESTING

Remove the bread from the oven and cool for at least one hour before slicing it. Bread that is just out of the oven continues to cook within and if sliced immediately, will have a gummy texture.

Notes: Don't feel bad about adding 1 teaspoon instant yeast to the flour mix if you are baking sourdough for the first few times, just as an added insurance that your bread turns out great. It will also give time for the starter to get more mature and dependable while you get started on your sourdough baking journey.

Chapter 3

Spice It Up

'*Each spice has a special day to it. For turmeric it is Sunday, when light drips fat and butter-coloured into the bins to be soaked up glowing, when you pray to the nine planets for love and luck.*'

—Chitra Banerjee Divakaruni

Before you dive into this chapter, I want you to do a little homework.

Count all the packets and bottles of whole spices, powdered spices and spice mixes from your kitchen shelves, fridge and freezer.

I did this homework too.

My score is fifty-six.

For a while, I worked in an office that was located in Vikhroli, a suburb of Mumbai. The second we stepped out of the air-conditioned confines of the office on to the road, we would be engulfed by the overpowering smell of masalas. The famous spice brand Everest had its factory in the vicinity. I have forgotten much about those days, but I still remember how strong the smell of spices in the air was. In India, spices surround us, permeating every aspect of our lives—cooking, health and even the air we breathe if we are close to a masala factory!

Working with spices is an art form. They are like tubes of oil paint in a box, and the possibilities you can create by combining them are limitless. The most vibrant colours come together to create a masterpiece in a Jamini Roy painting. Similarly, when we combine spices right, the dish created is nothing short of an edible art.

As Indians, most of us have access to this magic shelf in our kitchens that holds all the spices that we use in our everyday cooking. It would not be an exaggeration to say that spices are the all-important ingredient in Indian cooking. Even our sweet dishes cannot do without spices such as green cardamom, saffron and nutmeg.

Which spice to use, how much to use, how to coax more flavour out of them, what combinations work well and what doesn't work well, what spice makes a good home remedy, which is the best season to stock up on a particular spice—there is so much to be understood about spices.

Our great-grandmothers and grandmothers have learnt the usage of spices through heuristics. This heirloom knowledge has trickled down to us through observation and word of mouth. Storing whole spices for the entire year, preparing dry and wet spice mixes to flavour dishes, using a combination of spices as home remedies—the elders in our family are a treasure trove of this knowledge that we often take for granted. There aren't too many takers in our present generation who want to delve deep into making these spice mixes from scratch.

Brands, supermarkets and now online shopping have spoiled us for choice when it comes to spices and related products. We can order sandwich masala from a store in Vadodara, chhole masala from Kanpur and amchoor from Delhi at the touch of a phone screen.

I do understand that most of the complex masalas such as chhole, pav bhaji and chaat are best bought. Each such masala contains a long list of ingredients— it would be wasteful and time-consuming to buy each of these in small quantities and make sure to use them up before they lose potency or get infested.

On the other hand, sambar or rasam masala (podi), pizza and pasta sauce, pesto, kashundi, flavoured oils, molaga podi (gunpowder for idlis and dosas) and coriander and cumin powder are simpler to make at home. Besides, these freshly ground spices and condiments add a remarkable flavour to food that stale spices from a packet cannot achieve.

When I like a certain flavour in a packaged food or pickle, I try and replicate it at home by using the ingredient list on the packaging label as a guide. A couple of examples are the Grand Sweets tomato thokku (tomato pickle) and the masala that goes into the Mukharochak brand jhal muri. Both have such addictive flavours, and it is obvious that the secret lies in the spices. I have prepared both at home approximating the ingredients on the label and was happy with the results. Try this on some of your favourite spice mixes and see if the result matches the original!

The ability to eyeball the right quantity of spices to arrive at a desired flavour comes with years of cooking. That said, it also helps to develop an intuition around quantities of spices to be used and how to treat each spice when amateur cooks do this experiment on a regular basis.

Spices in different forms and storage conditions have different levels of aroma and flavour.

The aroma and flavour in ascending order:

- Pre-ground packaged spices kept at room temperature
- Pre-ground packaged spices kept in the fridge
- Pre-ground packaged spices kept in the freezer
- Freshly ground spices in an electric mixer just before cooking
- Freshly ground spices by hand just before cooking

How you use spices also determines the level of flavour extracted from them. Using spices whole gives a mild flavour, crushing them coarsely gives moderate flavour and a fine powder gives the maximum flavour hit. Finely ground spice powders also tend to lose flavour quickly as the aroma molecules are highly volatile. The level of flavour desired from a spice also depends on the dish you are cooking. Not every dish may need the full-on blast of finely powdered spices.

Spice Facts

The word 'spice' is derived from the Latin word 'species', which means an item of special value.

75 per cent of the spices in the world are grown in India.

In India, spices are not just used for cooking but also in home remedies for minor ailments, religious and cultural rituals, in cosmetics and for their essential oils that are used in perfumes, soaps, etc.

Spices are, in fact, plant defences. Thorny plants, plants growing high off the ground, plants with thick skins around the stems are all examples of physical defences to prevent us from eating plants. The chemical defences are far more complex. There is a concentration of toxic chemicals in different plant parts to prevent predators from eating them. These poisons are our spices. This very defence quality of spices comes into use when it protects cooked food from bacterial or fungal spoilage.

It is also the reason South-east Asian countries have a phenomenal variety of spices growing wild. Hotter weather in the tropics makes plants develop stronger defence mechanisms and store more toxins in the form of spices. This is also the science behind using whole cloves or bay leaves in boxes of dals or rice to keep pest infestation away. Cloves tied in a small square of muslin cloth (potli) can be kept inside almost all the dry provision boxes that tend to catch worms or other insects in our tropical weather conditions.

(continued)

An article in the *New York Times* (5 July 1995) titled 'The Power of Spices Ground Fresh' explains how almost all spices originated and are still widely grown in the narrow geographic band around the equator in tropical Asia. Due to ready availability, the people in this region 'learnt over generations of trial and error how best to use the multitude of barks, flowers, berries, roots, buds and seeds that make up the spice lexicon.'

Spices are also known for their food-preserving qualities, although whether they were used in food purely for preservation is questionable. For one, they were extremely expensive, and salt was always a much cheaper way to preserve food. There is a theory that suggests that in temperate climates, the colder weather meant less chance of spoilage, which is why fewer spices were used in the food. The food was automatically preserved in the sub-zero winter temperatures. It is the reason why Scandinavian food is so low on spices even to this date, while Indian food uses a variety of spices, even though we no longer have to use spices as a food preservative but purely for flavour.

How to Store Spices

This is one of the most important aspects of dealing with spices in order to preserve their flavour and aroma. It makes me wonder how spices were transported and stored in the early days. Whole spices were one of the earliest food products to be transported around the world, which tells us about their hardy quality. While the aroma or flavour deteriorates over time, whole spices hardly ever spoil. Initially, the spice trade from Asia and Africa to Europe was for spiritual, religious, aromatic or medicinal purposes and not primarily for food, so a loss of some percentage of flavour was not noticeable. Spices were transported in burlap sacks, which is a breathable fabric, so changes in temperature during transport did not cause condensation and moisture accumulation in the packed spices.

Today, whole spices are commercially sold in vacuum-sealed plastic pouches. If you tend to buy larger quantities of spices, always buy them whole. These have the longest shelf life. Mere application of mild heat can wake up the essential oils that are in the dormant state.

Keeping your spice jars near the cooking stove might seem like the most practical approach, but it's the one thing you should not do. Nothing denatures spices faster than heat, rendering them flavourless and bland. Keep only a small quantity in bottles for daily use. The Indian masala *dabba* (*anjarai petti* in Tamil) with five or seven cups to hold the everyday spices used in tempering or curries is the most scientific way to keep a small quantity of spices that are used many times a day within easy reach. Larger quantities are to be stored in airtight bottles in a cool, dry cabinet that is not next to the cooking range or stove.

Ground spices last six months, while whole spices can be used for five years. Spices don't have an expiry date but they do lose flavour over time, and you may need to use a larger quantity of the same spice if it is rather old.

Seed spices like sesame seeds and poppy seeds if not used regularly should be kept in the fridge or freezer to prevent them from going rancid.

The Life of Spices

Whole spices and herbs
Leaf/flower (bay leaf, star anise): 1 to 2 years
Seed/bark (ajwain, cinnamon, mustard seed): 2 to 3 years
Roots: 3 years
Ground spices and herbs
Leaves (dried mint powder): 1 year
Seed/bark (cinnamon powder, cumin powder): 1 year
Roots: 2 years

Why Prepare Spice Powders and Mixes at Home?

Apart from being a fulfilling experience in the kitchen with a free aromatherapy session thrown in from the rich fragrances of spices, here are some important reasons why you should make most spice mixes and condiments at home.

No fillers

Store-bought varieties of spice powders and condiments have a lot of cheap fillers like coriander seeds in garam masala and possibly pumpkin puree in tomato sauce. When made at home, these spice mixes and sauces can be created using fresh, seasonal and organic ingredients and no preservatives, added flavouring or colours.

High flavour

Home-made spice mixes or condiments are the easiest way to add much more flavour to food. There's a world of difference between the flavour of freshly ground black pepper versus black pepper powder from a shaker. The same goes for freshly grated nutmeg. Toasting spices like cumin or coriander seeds over low heat for two to three minutes intensifies flavours by waking up the volatile oils. The toasted seeds, when ground, yield a most aromatic spice powder.

No risk of adulteration

Spice powders from non-reputed brands or bought loose could also be adulterated using a variety of substances like sawdust powder, brick powder, chalk powder, starch and artificial colours. Adulteration can be done to increase the weight of the spice powder with cheap or non-edible ingredients, or to make them look brighter in colour. In most cases, it is not possible to identify adulteration using sight, smell or taste. Adulterants can range from harmless ingredients to potentially carcinogenic chemicals like metanil yellow and lead chromate, which are used to dye turmeric. When buying spices, always try to buy them whole as the chances of adulteration are negligible. If buying powdered spices or spice mixes, always look for the Agriculture Mark (AGMARK) logo and the

Food Safety and Standards Authority of India (FSSAI) licence number. In India, FSSAI has banned the sale of powdered spices in loose form.

No preservatives

You might have noticed how store-bought ketchup or pickle stays forever (unless you use a wet spoon, of course) even if left on the counter for months. It indicates that they are ultra-processed, full of preservatives, high in salt or sugar or both, and the ingredient list on the label will tell you that they have a whole bunch of things we don't identify as food.

Custom-made

Condiments like sauces and ketchup when made at home can be customized to suit your family's dietary requirements, for example, low sugar, no sugar, vegan, gluten free, dairy-free, etc. You can also make these with the best-quality organic ingredients for a fraction of the cost that they are sold for commercially.

The next best thing to making it yourself is to support local businesses that make such products in small batches, taking care to use the best available ingredients and adding no nasties.

Choosing a Spice Grinder

Now that you are all set to make your own spice powders and mixes, let us look at the implements that are useful for this purpose.

Mortar and pestle

These are available in stone, wood, ceramic or metals such as bronze. They are useful for grinding a small quantity of spices such as crushing ginger or cardamom for tea or crushing a few cloves of garlic and ginger for ginger garlic paste. It is not the chosen grinder when it comes to grinding larger quantities of any spices. Also, it is easier to crush hard spices like black pepper or cumin to a coarse powder using a mortar and pestle, but not relatively softer spices like dried red chillies.

The mortar and pestle is useful for dry grinding a small quantity of toasted spices for dishes like Indian curries because it grinds without generating heat that an electric mixer does, which causes some loss of flavour.

Amikal or *sil batta*

This is another hand-powered spice grinding set-up comprising a flat rough stone and a heavy cylindrical stone. This set used to be a part of most Indian kitchens, even embedded into the counter space in some, but has been phased out in favour of the quicker and low-effort electric mixer. It is used for both dry and wet grinding. Sil battas are now making a comeback in a small way for those who like hand-ground masalas in their cooking. These things being available on Amazon these days is a good indicator of the demand, don't you think?

Electric spice grinders

A spice grinder, also called a coffee grinder, is a very small mixer with around a half-cup capacity. The coffee grinder is to grind coffee beans for those who like to brew their cup from freshly ground beans. The subtle difference pointed out by connoisseurs is that the coffee grinders use conical burrs to grind the beans while spice grinders use blades.

If you do use your spice or coffee grinder interchangeably to grind coffee beans and spices, then the best way to remove any traces of other aromas from your grinder is to grind ½ cup of raw rice in it. This leaves the grinder clean and odour-free so your coffee does not smell of curry.

Small mixer jar called 'chutney jar attachment' of your regular mixer also works as good as the spice grinder. Just that the latter set-up is more compact to have around on the kitchen counter.

The best way to grind spices is to lightly toast them as applying heat releases their essential oils, making them more aromatic. Almost like waking up the dried spices from their slumber. Allowing the toasted spices to cool makes them crisp. These are easy to grind in a spice grinder to the level of fineness desired for the recipe. Care should be taken not to roast spices at a high temperature or roast them for too long as it may denature some of the flavour molecules, giving a somewhat undesirable bitter flavour.

In Tamil cooking, spices like red chillies, cumin seeds and black pepper are also fried in oil until crisp and aromatic and then ground with grated coconut for a fresh spice mix to go into kootu-like (a combination of cooked dals with vegetables) dishes.

Other equipment

A small cast iron pan is a good investment to dry-roast spices. Cast iron gets heated slowly and spreads the heat to the ingredients uniformly and gradually.

A small coir brush is nice to have, to stir the spices for even roasting over a low flame.

Four Must-Have Flavour Bombs

While these four ingredients are not spices in the true sense of the word, given that they add intense flavour to dishes, I am going to address them as spices here.

These four ground spices, when added to your masala mix, gives it an added boost of flavour, something you will find in the readymade mixes or the flavour sachets of instant noodles packets. Each of the following spice powders packs great depth of flavour, but when added to four or five other spices gives the mixture that hint of mystery, something that people love when they eat.

Onion powder

Onion powder is made from dehydrated onions. Commercially available onion powder is around ten times stronger in flavour than fresh onions. It is an important ingredient in pasta and pizza seasoning, commercially prepared ketchup and soup sachets. At home, you can use onion powder to prepare your own seasonings, rubs and even salad dressings.

Onion salt is made by combining five parts of onion powder with one part of salt. This can be sprinkled on pizzas, pasta or home-made popcorn.

Onion powder can be made at home by sun-drying thinly sliced onions spread out in a single layer on a cloth or baking trays for three or four days until dried to a crisp. A dehydrator makes it easy to dry fresh ingredients. These dried onion slices are ground to a powder. Onion powder is best stored in an airtight jar in the fridge as it is prone to caking and spoilage when left at higher room temperatures. The anti-caking agent calcium silicate is usually added to the powder in commercially sold onion powder.

Garlic powder

This seasoning lends the flavour of garlic to savoury dishes without the extra effort of peeling and chopping garlic cloves. It is the best way to add garlic flavour to seasoning mixes combined with salt, dried herbs, chilli flakes and onion powder. Kept in airtight bottles, garlic powder has a long shelf life of three to four years, but exposure to moisture and higher room temperatures makes it clump up. Buy smaller bottles and keep them refrigerated if you live in a hot place.

Add garlic powder to soups, salad dressings, grilled cheese sandwiches, potato subzi and more. To make garlic salt, combine three parts garlic powder with one part salt by volume. Garlic salt is a delicious topping on most savoury snacks like popcorn, chivda (Indian puffed rice snack) or pizza.

Black salt

Black salt is not a true salt but a combination of minerals in crystal form, with a sulphur-like aroma. This is one of the ingredients that brings umami to vegetarian food, especially chaats. There's no reason why you should not replace some of the salt used in a dish with black salt.

It is the most important ingredient in chaat masala, made by combining roasted cumin powder for its smokiness, crushed pomegranate seeds (anardana) and amchoor for tang, ground black pepper for heat and black salt for the characteristic flavour. Some recipes for chaat masala include dried mint powder, coriander powder, ground ajwain and garam masala in addition to the above-mentioned spices.

Black salt alone can be sprinkled over cut fruits to markedly improve their flavour.

Kasuri methi

Methi or fenugreek leaves are a winter season leafy green in north India. Their mildly bitter flavour adds an unmistakable aroma to dal, gravies, dry subzis or flatbreads like thepla. When fresh methi is in season, buy large bunches and pluck the leaves. Wash well and gently pat dry using a cotton towel. These leaves can be microwaved in batches to get dried methi or kasuri methi. Simply spread out the leaves in one layer on the glass revolving plate of the microwave and run on 60 per cent power for one to two minutes in thirty-second bursts until the leaves are dried to a crisp.

You can also buy ready-made kasuri methi. Storing it in the freezer retains the aroma best, and it's also easy to crush it into a fine powder using fingertips before adding to a dish. In north Indian dishes like dal makhani or paneer in gravy, kasuri methi adds a buttery, delicious flavour. It is one flavour bomb of a spice that you absolutely must stock in the kitchen.

Make your own seasoning blends at home using flavour bomb spice powders. These make lovely gifts.

Seasoning blend	Quality	Components
Za'taar	Bitter, warm	Thyme/oregano, sesame seeds, sumac, salt
Herbs de Provence	Herby, earthy	Marjoram, oregano, rosemary, sage, tarragon, thyme
Chinese five spice	Warming, sweet	Cassia, clove, fennel, star anise, Sichuan peppercorns
Cajun	Spicy, earthy	Black peppercorns, paprika, red chilli, cumin, thyme
Moroccan ras el hanout	Sweet, spicy	Cardamom, clove, cinnamon, paprika, coriander, cumin, nutmeg, black peppercorns, turmeric

Middle Eastern seven spice mix	Sweet, smoky	Black peppercorns, cardamom, cinnamon, cloves, coriander, cumin, nutmeg, smoked paprika

Other Condiments That You Should Try Using Spices

Spices add flavour not just to curries and pickles. Using a select few spices in any dish can lift its flavour profile and make it more appetizing.

Flavoured or infused oils

The best way to finish a dish is to make the aroma of spices linger on the surface of the bowl, and make your mouth water. Flavoured or infused oils are a great way to do this. They can be made using any oil and a combination of any spices reflective of a certain cuisine. For example, red chillies, curry leaves, garlic, black pepper, cumin seeds and asafoetida in gingelly oil for a Tamil flavour. For an Italian flavour, try garlic, dried basil, lemon zest in olive oil.

Salad dressings

Dressings are great carriers for spices, which act as flavour-boosting agents. To the base of extra virgin olive oil, lemon juice (or a vinegar) and salt, adding one or two spices makes the salad dressing all the more flavourful. Some of the spices that can be used in a salad dressing are freshly crushed black pepper, roasted cumin powder, toasted sesame seeds, chilli flakes, carom seeds, ground turmeric and ground mustard seeds.

Condiments from around the world

Spices are the soul of not just chutneys and pickles but also condiments such as tomato ketchup, hot sauce, sweet chilli sauce, barbecue sauce and chili oil. By changing up the spice combinations used, you can come up with a variety of condiments using the same recipes.

Rubs and marinades

Some examples of dry rubs are coffee rub on steak, turmeric marinades for fish, jerk marinade for chicken and Japanese-style seasoning salt. These work best on meat or seafood-based dishes. Marinades made using chilli flakes, sesame seeds, grated ginger and soy sauce work well for tofu or as a drizzle over grilled eggplants. The dry rubs and marinades can be prepared in larger quantities for gifting or regular use in cooking.

Spice-infused alcohols and vinegars

Alcohols are great for extracting maximum flavour out of spices, herbs or a combination of the two. White spirits like vodka, white rum and gin are good for infusing. Stronger spices like chillies and vanilla release their flavour and aroma in just twenty-four hours while other spices take up to a week. Spices are filtered out using a cheesecloth-lined sieve after the infusing period. Infused alcohol is shelf-stable for a very long time, although the spice flavour may mellow with time. Chilli vodka and star anise gin are just some of the possibilities to explore.

Spice-infused vinegars are good to give a final spritz of freshness to a dish or even for use in salad dressings. Chillies, fresh black pepper corns and star anise are some of the ingredients that can be used to prepare infused vinegars. These vinegars can be used in salad dressings or in a small quantity to add acidity and flavour to any other dish.

Podi

Podis in south Indian cuisine are a wonderful way to use spices in everyday meals. Podi, meaning powder in Tamil, is usually had with hot rice and ghee. But let that not limit you from using it in multiple ways.

1. Top your avocado toast with podi for flavour and crunch.
2. Mix it with oil and have it with any of the Indian breakfasts or snacks.
3. Add to savoury yoghurt bowls or porridge.
4. Sprinkle inside masala parathas or spread a podi-oil mixture inside the paratha layers before rolling it out.
5. Add to mashed potatoes for a unique flavour.

Spices as a Business

There is a growing demand for good-quality spices, spice mixes, artisanal family recipes for condiments and pickles. Customers are willing to pay extra for good-quality products. If you are passionate about spices and would like to start a business around spices, here are a few avenues to consider.

1. Focus on sourcing high-quality spices from farmers and start your own line. This could be whole spices, powdered spices or blends. You can also focus on just one spice like pepper or turmeric and make that your forte. Once the business picks up you can include more spices on your list.

2. Export high-quality spices to other countries. India is known for its variety and quality of spices. Exporting Indian-grown spices to countries where there is demand is one of the business options.

3. With the ready-to-cook market growing in leaps, developing curry pastes for Asian curries using the best quality ingredients is another idea.

4. Spice-centred condiments such as infused oils, vinegars, salad dressings, pickles, chutneys, podis are all ideas for product lines. Focus on one or two categories to start with and expand gradually.

5. Spices extracted in spirits like vodka and gin to create an artisanal line of spirits for use in cocktails (for example, vanilla vodka, jalapeno gin) or creating cocktail premixes with fresh juices and spices are some of the options to explore in the beverage industry.

6. Extracts of spices (oleoresins) such as ginger, green cardamom, lemongrass and chai masala are popular these days as spice drops to add to your cup of tea. It is an easy way to customize each cup of tea by adding a drop of this extract using a dropper.

Interview with Mallika Basu of SIZL Spices

Mallika Basu is the founder of SIZL Spices, a food writer with two published cookbooks—*Miss Masala: Real Indian Cooking for Busy Living* and *Masala: Indian Cooking for Modern Living*, a media commentator and columnist. Born and brought up in Kolkata, India, she has had a long career in the public relations (PR) and communications industry alongside which she developed a speciality in writing about wholesome recipes, bold flavours and easy cheats for today's modern kitchen. When not cooking, Mallika runs a 'business of food' consultancy advising the industry on diversity and inclusion, cultural sensitivity, brand strategy and marketing, food writing, product development, and the role of food and drink in economic regeneration.

Tell us about yourself, Mallika.

I'm a single parent, co-parenting my two kids with my ex-husband who is also the business partner in my spice business. I run two businesses—a spice business and a food consultancy.

When did you start cooking and who was your inspiration?

I started cooking just as I was finishing my undergrad degree. I started cooking regularly when doing my masters in the UK. I realized if I wanted *ghar ka khana*, I had no option but to make it myself. I would play with ingredients, call my mom, granny and dad, who are all great cooks and my inspirations.

As a PR professional, how did the idea for a food blog come along and then the books?

When I told my friends that I was going to start a food blog, they gave each other 'the look'. I started teaching myself Indian cooking and documenting my trials on my food blog. It was named *Quick Indian Cooking* because I was trying to address the Western perception that Indian food takes hours to cook and that it's very complicated and greasy. If a twenty-something PR professional with a busy family and social life like me can cook Indian food, then anybody can.

I loved writing, I had trained as a journalist at the *Asian Age* in Kolkata. I loved my work in communications. I wasn't one of those people who hated their day job. I was out with a friend at a pub, when we hit upon the idea for the blog design. Blogs were a very fresh thing at that time, and my blog did very well in a short period. A friend in publishing helped me get an agent who then got me my first book deal. Both the blog and the book struck a chord with the audience.

How did you think of getting started with the spice business?

When I started my blog, I considered it as a creative outlet. Even though it gathered an eager audience, my intention was never to make money from the blog.

I was looking for a way to monetize my interest and passion for food, as people were interested in what I had to say. I would often get asked, 'Where do you get your spices from?' I was generally underwhelmed with the spices and spice blends available in the UK.

This led me to invest all my savings in a spice business and, unfortunately, I lost most of it in 2010. While I had written two cookbooks, they don't generate an income you can live on. An opportunity came up to collaborate with a spice expert who was running an organic wholesale spice business. He wanted to come into the retail space. My ex-husband put the two of us together and he himself came on as creative director. Another partner who oversaw ops and logistics. The four of us got together to make SIZL Spices. Although I understand business and marketing, I had never done a product line before. This was a completely new thing for me.

What are the first few products you started with and how was the expansion journey? How did you decide on what products to start with and which ones to expand into?

We started with a range of sixteen single tins. The idea was that it would launch along with my second cookbook, so we launched after Diwali in 2019. We were just finding our feet and the pandemic happened. We saw good sales in that period. People were spending a lot more time on home cooking. During the lockdown, home cooks were coming up with a lot of recipes, and it was tough to find half the ingredients, which were getting sold out. To help home cooks and take away some of the stress from cooking, we launched five multi-use spice blends. We started low key in pouches, then we found a retailer who loved them. The retailer helped us redesign the packaging to be more shelf ready. The response so far has been great. My fingers are crossed for a massive launch in the shops.

In India, if someone wants to get into a spices and condiments business, what are your tips or advice for them—what to start with, how to look for a gap in the market?

I am a big fan of indigenous spice mixes from all over India. There is a huge market and opportunity as the mixes vary as per family and community. For example, garam masala from Kolkata versus Delhi versus Kerala, each of them has its own nuances and usage.

One needs to understand the difference between selling a product versus selling a brand. When you create your brand, you get the economy of scale and scope, and you can charge a higher margin—for example, a sachet of spice packaged in a clear pouch with a sticker versus a brand name that means something.

Things work best in threes. Come up with the top three things that you and your brand stand for. It could be something like 'your grandmother's recipe that's worked for years'. For example, at SIZL Spices, our USP is that we don't add any fillers. I strongly feel that unless sugar or salt has a purpose, it should not be part of a blend. Customers shouldn't be paying for salt and sugar in a spice blend.

If you want to take the business to the next level, create a brand, look at the packaging, get the messaging right, go for something you can be the best at. As the saying in communications goes, if you can't be the first, be the best.

Is there a lot of upfront investment in the spice business?

I think it is entirely possible to start with a small investment. The trickier thing is to grow and get the product into shops. With online retailing and Amazon-like marketplaces, the route to the market has become much more affordable and easier.

Keep your primary source of income going to invest in the business and build as you go along.

How much effort, time and money go into branding, design and packaging, and how early or late in the small business journey should one invest in this?

It depends on the product and range of products and how much money you're making. In spices, there's a limit to the margins you can have. Don't spend a whole lot of money upfront; test the market and see what people are responding to.

What is more important is to have an end goal in mind and getting under the skin of the market, understanding what the customers want. People are brand loyal when it comes to a spice mix. Building that following and customer loyalty is more important. There's a lot more to marketing than just Instagram numbers.

Our single spice that sells the most is mustard seeds, which I would not have guessed. Don't start with a massive range. Start small, test it and keep tweaking. Grow it from what you've learnt. Don't work with lots of expensive agencies and third parties. Keep costs tight. Get things done well, but don't go off on a spending spree, as it takes time to build revenues.

How easy or difficult it is to get shelf space in supermarket chains?

It is extremely difficult here in the UK because the system has a lot of complicated processes, and it is a competitive space. I've stressed out the most over this more than anything else. Cutting through the competition and getting to the shelf space is tough. Look into that process before you get started as you need to understand how that works.

Should new businesses look to sell online or from brick-and-mortar shops?

I'm a big fan of DTC, as you can connect with your audience and learn from them. But you do need someone to package, distribute, handle customer complaints, someone needs to plug in online sales channels and brand interfaces. There is no right or wrong answer to this, it depends on your end goal. Work backwards from there.

What are some other skills you need to hone to set up this business?

Marketing is essential and understanding this is vital. The product that doesn't sell is worth nothing.

Brand awareness, marketing and sales are three different things. Get good at all three. Softer skills like listening and being efficient are also important. Someone who is good with finances is a must-have on the team, to make sure there is a tight lid on spends, that the margins are right. Outsource this if you don't have this skill set.

Your favourite spice mixes—Indian and international?

Garam masala, sambar masala and a xacuti masala I picked up from Mapusa market in Goa.

International ones are baharat, Lebanese seven-spice, yellow bean paste, gochujang and harissa.

Projects

After that deep dive into spices, I'm sure you cannot wait to try some of these projects. I have included a variety of versatile recipes that will add much flavour to any dish.

1. A Quartet of Flavour Bomb Seasonings   108
2. A Trio of Podis   110
3. The Infused Oils Trilogy   115
4. Your New Favourite Mustard Sauce: Aam Kashundi   118
5. The All-Purpose Satay Sauce   119
6. Schezwan Sauce/Chilli Garlic Sauce   120
7. Pineapple Ginger Chutney   121
8. Salted Caramel Sauce   123

1. A Quartet of Flavour Bomb Seasonings

These seasoning mixes feature either onion powder, garlic powder, black salt or kasuri methi, for their unmistakable deep flavour. Experiment with the spice powders and herbs in your kitchen to make your signature spice mixes. Mix the ingredients in a clean, dry bowl and spoon it into airtight bottles. Don't forget to stick a pretty label on the bottle. These make for beautiful gifts too.

Italian seasoning

Use it in pastas, to season oven roasted vegetables and in salad dressings.

Combine:
2 tbsp dried basil
2 tbsp dried oregano
2 tbsp dried rosemary
2 tbsp dried thyme
2 tbsp dried parsley
2 tsp garlic powder

Cajun seasoning

Use it to season baked potato wedges, oven-roasted vegetables, grilled chicken and dishes like gumbo.

Combine:
1 tbsp Kashmiri chilli powder
1 tbsp paprika powder
1 tbsp dried oregano
1 tbsp ground black pepper

1 tsp garlic powder
1 tsp onion powder
2 tbsp salt

Heart-friendly salt-free seasoning

The flavours of these spices more than make up for the salt. Fill this in a salt shaker and place it on your dining table to top any dishes with more flavour. Use on fried or scrambled eggs, omelettes, yoghurt, sliced raw vegetables like cucumbers, tomatoes and onions.

Combine:
1 tbsp garlic powder
2 tbsp onion powder
1 tbsp Kashmiri chilli powder
1 tbsp smoked paprika (or regular paprika)
1 tbsp dried oregano
1 tsp ground black pepper

Indian all-purpose seasoning

Use it to finish any curries or dals, or mix with some oil and smear on rolled out dough to make layered masala parathas.

Combine:
1 tbsp garlic powder
1 tsp black salt
1 tsp ground cumin
2 tsp amchoor powder
1 tbsp onion powder

1 tbsp ground coriander
1 tbsp Kashmiri chilli powder
1 tbsp crushed kasuri methi

2. A Trio of Podis

Paruppu Podi

Paruppu podi is a genius idea of having a ready-to-eat dal to go with rice without the hassle of actually cooking the dal. The secret is to have melted ghee or gingelly oil along with steaming hot rice so that the podi clings to every morsel of rice, flavouring it beautifully. A dry curry and papad on the side are all you need to make a comfort meal out of it. It is also great for vegetarians or vegans travelling to places where they are not sure of getting vegan food, or for students in hostels who only have access to a rice cooker. Make your own gourmet version of a paruppu podi with a variety of spices and it makes for a lovely food gift or care package.

Gather

1 tsp ghee
2 tsp whole black peppercorns
4–6 dried red chillies (mild or hot depending on your preference)
3–4 cloves of garlic (optional but adds good flavour)
1 cup tur dal
¼ cup fried gram (dalia/pottu kadalai)

1-½ tsp rock salt
Pinch of asafoetida

Make

In a heavy-bottomed pan, heat the ghee and add the black pepper, red chillies and garlic. Fry on a low flame for two to three minutes until the chillies are bright red and crisp. Remove this to a plate.

In the same pan, add the tur dal and roast for five to six minutes on a low flame until aromatic and a few shades darker. Don't let this become dark brown or get burnt as it will make the podi bitter. Remove this to the plate to cool.

Turn off the flame and add the fried gram, rock salt and asafoetida. Fry for a minute. Allow this to cool as well.

Once all the ingredients are cooled, transfer to a mixer jar and process to get a fine powder. Let the podi come to room temperature before storing it in an airtight container.

To eat, mix enough podi depending on the quantity of hot rice along with melted ghee or gingelly oil.

Notes: You can omit the fried gram and use tur dal alone.

You can also use up to 2 tbsp of flax seeds in this podi to add to its nutritional value. Dry roast the seeds separately until they start popping. Grind along with the remaining ingredients.

Molaga Podi

This spice and lentil powder is a standard accompaniment for idlis and dosas. The texture of this podi is a personal preference, much like peanut butter. I love it crunchy, which means the lentils need to be coarsely ground. Some find the coarse texture annoying and something that gets stuck in the teeth, in which case all you need to do is process it to a fine powder. The oil of choice to mix molaga podi in is gingelly oil (south Indian sesame oil), but melted coconut oil, ghee and yoghurt can also be used. Each family has their own recipe. Use any mix of split lentils and roast them until aromatic. Roast dried red chillies until crisp. Add other ingredients like sesame seeds, curry leaves or desiccated coconut and you can make your own variant of molaga podi.

Makes over 1 cup.

Gather

2 tsp gingelly oil
½ cup urad dal (split, skinned)
¼ cup tur dal
¼ cup chana dal
¼ cup white or black sesame seeds*
15–20 whole dried red chillies**
1–2 tsp rock salt

---

* Using black sesame seeds will give you a darker coloured podi.
** Reduce or increase the number depending on the heat in the chillies. Milder chillies like Byadagi are great for vibrant red colour and mild heat, while Guntur chillies are good for those who like it spicy.

Make

In a heavy-bottomed pan, heat around ½ tsp of oil. Add the urad dal and roast over a low flame for six to eight minutes until golden brown.

Remove to a plate and repeat the process with a few drops of oil with tur dal and then the chana dal. The idea behind roasting them separately is that the dals differ in size and the time taken to roast each one differs. Doing this process separately for each dal means that each of them will roast uniformly without burning. Remove all the roasted dals to a dish and keep them aside.

Now add the sesame seeds to the pan. Keep stirring. In a couple of minutes, the seeds will start popping. Remove to the dish once the popping stops.

Break or snip the dried red chillies into two or three pieces each. Heat a few drops of oil in the same pan and slow roast the chillies until they turn bright red and crisp. Allow all the ingredients to cool.

In a clean, dry mixer jar, add all the roasted ingredients (dals, sesame seeds, chillies) along with the salt. Use the pulse function four or five times for ten seconds each to get a coarse powder. Run the mixer at a high speed to get a fine powder. Store in an airtight container. This will stay good for around two months.

Curry Leaf Podi

This is the best gift to give a south Indian friend who is going abroad as curry leaves are not as easy to come by or as cheap as they are in India. Curry leaves used in tempering are often picked out and discarded. Using them in a podi ensures that all the nutritive goodness of this superfood is not wasted.

If you have a large curry leaf plant at home or a friend's house, this podi is best made when the tree or plant is pruned.

Gather

2 cups of curry leaves (packed)
½ cup urad dal (split, skinned)
¼ cup tur dal
4–6 dried red chillies (mild or spicy as per preference)
1 tsp cumin seeds
1 tsp black peppercorns
1 tsp rock salt

Make

Wash the curry leaves and dry them on an absorbent cotton towel.

Heat a heavy-bottomed pan. Roast the urad dal and tur dal one after another over a low flame for five to six minutes until they turn a few shades darker. Don't brown them. Remove to a dish to cool.

Dry roast the red chillies until they turn crisp and bright red. Remove to the dish.

Next, roast the cumin seeds and black pepper on a low flame for a minute or so, until aromatic.

Put the washed and dried curry leaves in the pan and dry roast for five to six minutes until the leaves turn crisp. They should crumble to a powder when crushed with your fingers. Don't let the leaves turn brown as this will affect the flavour and colour of the podi.

In a clean, dry mixer jar, add all the roasted ingredients along with the salt. Use the pulse function four or five times for ten seconds each to get a coarse powder. Run the mixer at a high speed to get a fine powder. Store in an airtight container. This will stay good for around two months, but the fragrance of curry leaves is best when consumed within a week or two.

To eat, combine the podi with hot rice and ghee.

3. The Infused Oils Trilogy

Asian Chilli Oil

This chilli oil elevates the flavour of almost every savoury dish and is perfect to drizzle on noodles, pasta, salads, grilled vegetables or eggs.

To make Asian-style chilli oil, heat half a cup of peanut oil. The oil must not reach a smoking hot level, but just short of that.

Allow it to cool for five minutes. Meanwhile, gather the ingredients that you must add to the oil.

Gather

1–2 tsp Sichuan peppercorns
3 tbsp chilli flakes (Korean gochugaru if you can find it)
½ tsp black peppercorns, crushed
1 tsp ground ginger

1 star anise
2 tsp toasted sesame oil

Make

Toast the Sichuan peppercorns lightly in a small pan. Once cooled, crush in a mortar and pestle to a coarse powder.

Add all the ingredients to the heated and slightly cooled peanut oil. Stir well using a spoon or chopstick. Pour into a glass bottle. The chilli oil can be used immediately but the flavour improves in two or three days.

Italian-Style Infused Oil

Use to make a delicious salad dressing, or add to pasta, pizza, grilled vegetables or eggs for an extra burst of flavour.

Gather

250 ml extra virgin olive oil
Peel of 1–2 limes
5–6 cloves garlic, peeled
A handful of fresh Italian basil leaves
3–4 sprigs of rosemary

Make

In a heavy pot, combine all the ingredients and let them heat on the lowest flame setting for fifteen minutes.

Cover and let the mixture continue to infuse for two to three hours.

Strain the oil into a jug and pour it into a glass bottle using a funnel. Keep this refrigerated and use within a month.

South Indian Infused Oil

You can use this as a finishing oil on sambar, kootu or kuzhambu-type dishes. You can also use it to mix molaga podi, drizzle it over raita or use as a salad dressing.

Gather

250 ml gingelly oil
1 tsp black peppercorns, slightly crushed
1 tsp cumin seeds
4–5 dried red chillies, broken
4 sprigs curry leaves (leaves stripped)
4–5 slices of ginger
5–6 cloves garlic, crushed
6–7 shallots, thinly sliced

Make

In a heavy pot, combine all the ingredients and let them heat on the lowest flame setting for fifteen minutes.

Cover and let them continue to infuse for two to three hours.

Strain the oil into a jug and pour it into a glass bottle using a funnel. Keep this refrigerated and use within a month.

4. Your New Favourite Mustard Sauce: Aam Kashundi

The highlight spice of this sauce is mustard seeds. A must-stock in your fridge when raw mangoes are in season, this condiment perks up the most basic of dal-rice meals with its pungent and piquant character.

Gather

1 tbsp each of black and yellow mustard seeds (soaked in water for one hour)
1 medium-sized raw mango, roughly chopped
3 cloves garlic
3 spicy green chillies
2 tbsp mustard oil
1–2 tbsp sugar
1 tsp salt

Make

Drain and blend the soaked mustard seeds along with raw mango, garlic, chillies, mustard oil, salt and sugar until thick and creamy.

Transfer this to a glass jar and pour another tablespoon of mustard oil on the top.

Keep this with a loose-fitting lid on the counter to ferment for one or two days. Then, close with an airtight lid and refrigerate. Use within two to three weeks.

5. The All-Purpose Satay Sauce

This makes for an excellent dipping sauce not just for Vietnamese spring rolls but for all kinds of starters. It is the perfect balance of all flavours. You can also use it as a dressing over roasted or grilled vegetables, or use it to dip crudités in.

Gather

½ cup peanut butter (creamy or crunchy, either is fine)
1 tbsp dark soy sauce
2–3 tbsp crushed jaggery
3 tbsp lime juice
1 tsp red chilli powder
3 cloves garlic
¼ cup water

Make

In a mixer jar, combine all the ingredients and blend to get a smooth sauce. Taste and adjust the ingredients for salt, spice, tanginess and sweetness as per your liking.

Instead of peanut butter, you can also use ½ cup roasted peanuts and blend it with the other ingredients until smooth.

6. Schezwan Sauce/Chilli Garlic Sauce

Use this to make chilli garlic noodles, rice, mushrooms or vegetables.

Makes 200 g.

Gather

30 dried Byadagi red chillies (30 g)
25 large cloves garlic (50 g)
3–4 tbsp sunflower oil
2 tbsp vinegar (white or malt)
1 tbsp dark soy sauce
1-½ tsp salt

Make

Remove the stems of the chillies. Wash and soak in a bowl of hot water for thirty minutes, weighing it down with a heavy plate so the chillies remain immersed in water. Chop the garlic finely. You can use a food processor for this.

Remove the rehydrated chillies to a mixer jar and blend to a smooth puree. Reserve the soaking water.

Combine the oil and chopped garlic in a pan. Stir to combine and then keep it on low heat. Stir continuously for five to six minutes, taking care that the garlic does not burn, until it no longer smells raw.

To this, add the chilli puree and bring it to a simmer. Continue cooking this mixture for three or four minutes. It will splutter, so keep partially covered with a lid.

At this point, add the vinegar, soy sauce and salt, along with ½ cup of the reserved chilli-soaking water. Simmer this on a low flame for eight to ten minutes until the oil separates.

Once cooled, pour it into a clean, dry glass jar. It will stay in the refrigerator for eight to ten days.

7. Pineapple Ginger Chutney

Makes around 500 g.

Many people cannot tolerate eating pineapple as is, as it affects their throat. Enjoy the delicious flavours of pineapple in this spice-infused chutney. It makes for a lovely addition to a brunch platter along with sourdough breads and cheese, or plain and simple on buttered toast. The chutney also tastes great with parathas.

Gather

1 tbsp cold pressed mustard oil
2 tsp nigella seeds
1 tsp cumin seeds
1 kg ripe pineapple, diced small (see the canned option in Notes)
100 g finely chopped ginger
100 g golden raisins
4 green chillies, minced
250 g raw cane sugar
2 tbsp salt

2 tsp black salt
250 ml apple cider vinegar (or any other natural fruit vinegar)
1 tbsp onion powder
1 tbsp garlic powder
2 tsp cumin powder

Make

In a large pot, heat the oil. Fry the nigella seeds and cumin seeds for a few seconds.

Add all the remaining ingredients to the pot and let it come to a boil. Check for salt and sugar and adjust it as per your liking.

Reduce the flame and simmer for around forty-five minutes until the pineapple is mushy.

Stir continuously towards the end to prevent the chutney from sticking to the bottom of the pot.

While the chutney is getting ready, sterilize a 1-litre capacity bottle. Wash with soap and hot water, drain thoroughly. Place on a baking tray and keep inside a preheated oven at 125°C for thirty minutes. Sterilize the lids by placing them in boiling water for ten minutes. Wipe the bottles and lids thoroughly using a clean kitchen towel. Spoon the chutney into the bottles.

Notes: To use canned pineapple instead of fresh, select one that is not preserved in sugar syrup. The weight of the drained pineapple slices or bits should be 700–800 g.

8. Salted Caramel Sauce

The one sauce that elevates almost any dessert is salted caramel sauce. When made at home, you can flavour it with a splash of bourbon, dark rum or whisky. Drizzle the insides of a glass with this sauce to serve iced lattes or frappes for a café-style finish. It makes for a great Christmas gift.

Gather

¾ cup sugar
6 tbsp salted butter, cubes
½ cup cream
1 tsp rock salt

Make

Take the sugar in a heavy-bottomed pan. On low to medium heat, allow the sugar to melt and then turn a few shades darker, turning it into caramel. Lightly swirl the pan to distribute the heat through the caramel.

Once it is amber, gently add the cubes of butter, stirring continuously.

After the butter has melted and mixed well with the caramel, add the cream and salt and mix gently. Simmer for one or two minutes and remove the pan from heat.

Once it has cooled, transfer to a clean, dry glass jar. Refrigerate and use within two or three weeks.

Chapter 4

Get Fizzy

'Fermentation and civilization are inseparable.'
—John Ciardi

Where there is life, there is fermentation.

Microorganisms are intimately related to human life. Unlike the womb, the birth canal is teeming with bacteria. The journey of a baby from the womb to the outside world through the birth canal gives it the first dose of microbes. The baby's microbiome continues to be nurtured by the mother's milk, which was earlier thought to be sterile. Breast milk also feeds the existing gut bacteria in the baby, kickstarting the baby's fledgling immune and digestive systems. Our first brush with bacteria continues into the rest of our life, until death and beyond.

A study was published in the *Proceedings of the National Academy of Sciences* on a fascinating census sorting all the life on earth by weight. The weight of bacteria on the planet is 1200 times more than the weight of all the humans on the planet. They are omnipresent, on our skin, inside our bodies and on the surface of all vegetables and fruits. When humans channelize the power of bacteria and fungi to benefit us, add flavour to food and modify food in a way we seek, it is called fermentation.

The process of fermentation allows bacteria and fungi to break down complex sugars from cane, fruits, vegetables, dairy or any other starches into simple, easily digestible components, thereby generating new compounds and flavours. As humans, we can convert any ingredient that is given to us into a dish, but the molecular breakdown that happens during fermentation is doable only by microorganisms in cooperation with time.

Why should you ferment?

1. It is fairly simple, and you don't need a degree in biochemistry to figure out how to ferment foods. By fermentation, we are harnessing the bacteria and yeast to do the cooking for us, pre-digesting food, creating flavours in a way we cannot do ourselves in the kitchen and providing more bioavailable nutrients.

2. Fermented foods are less prone to spoilage because harmful pathogens cannot survive in the acidic environment. It was used as a

method to preserve food for longer when there was no access to refrigeration and other food-preserving technology.

3. Using fermentation, we can make a variety of lacto-fermented beverages like whey sodas and ginger ales at home, reducing our dependence on artificially flavoured and highly sugary drinks. These are not only low in sugar but have no artificial colours, preservatives or additives. Seasonal fruits, herbs, spices and pretty much any other natural produce can be used in these beverages. Home-made lacto-fermented beverages are also low in alcohol content, making a good replacement for alcoholic drinks for those who are keen to cut down on alcohol.

4. Eating fermented food regularly helps maintain a good gut microbiome. Gut bacteria play an important role in immunity, mental health, digestion, regulating blood sugar and cholesterol levels, and more. The majority of commercial 'probiotic' supplements don't survive stomach acid. A thriving gut microbiome requires a regular intake of fermented foods and foods containing resistant starch (for example, raw papaya, plantain, beans and legumes, cooked and cooled rice or potatoes) that feed the good bacteria in the large intestine. Regular consumption of fermented foods also helps ease gut-related problems like acidity, bloating and poor digestion.

5. Homemade ferments have a microbial diversity that commercially made, bottled fermented drinks lack, as they are inoculated with a set quantity of known strains. This is understandable as a

fixed quantity of known microbes will give a predictable result and the standardization that commercial brands need.

6. Fermentation makes vegetables fun. Raw carrots that are tooth-breakingly hard do very well with three days of lacto-fermentation. It is a great way to snack on carrots with hummus, or you can simply dice these and add to salads for a beautiful flavour profile. The brine can also be drunk diluted in water as a digestive beverage as it is full of beneficial bacteria.

7. Fermentation is a step towards zero waste where excess produce can be preserved for longer or kitchen waste such as the peels, pith and seeds of fruits like pineapple, mango, apples, etc. can be used to make sodas and vinegar.

To sum up, fermented foods are beneficial to the gut and overall well-being. Fermentation helps reduce food waste, adds a ton of flavour to our dishes, gives us an array of refreshing home-made beverages and a number of condiment options to play with. It is like having a chemistry lab in your kitchen. Once you start, you won't be able to stop experimenting.

Understanding Some Basics of Fermentation

Lacto-fermentation, one of the most common processes followed in fermenting food, happens due to lactobacillus, a species of bacteria. It was named thus because this bacteria was first studied in milk ferments. It is not to be mistaken as associated with dairy.

Different strains of this species are found on the surfaces of all plants, more so in those growing closer to the ground or underground. They are also present in the human gastrointestinal tract, mouth and vagina. It is something that truly connects humans with the soil, the produce and everything around us.

In lacto-fermentation, bacteria, fungi, yeast or mould break down the carbohydrates or sugars in food into acids, gas and alcohol. Lacto-fermentation is always an anaerobic process. The produce you want to lacto-ferment has to be well submerged under brine and the bottle capped with a lid.

Almost any produce can be lacto-fermented. The process improves flavour, extends shelf life and offers health benefits by providing beneficial bacteria to the gut.

This method of fermentation gives you a new way to deal with the same old vegetables and fruits. Lacto-fermented pickles, for example, are neither raw nor cooked, but mildly worked upon by the fascinating bacteria that break down the sugars in the produce, giving you a product with a lot more interesting flavour.

Cut hard vegetables like carrots, beets and radish into batons and arrange snugly in a bottle. Top with water and the required quantity of salt. Add in any flavouring spices like mustard seeds or black pepper. Close the lid, making sure that all the vegetables are submerged. Keep it for around a week and you'll have crunchy veggies that are tangy and delicious.

Sugar or starch in the starting materials can either remain as is or turn into lactic acid, alcohol or acetic acid.

Glucose is a simple sugar. Bacteria or yeast can break down sugar into two molecules of lactic acid, which is sour to taste. This is what makes sugar-sweetened beverages tangy when lactic acid fermentation happens.

Some of the lactic acid gets further broken down into ethanol (alcohol) along with carbon dioxide, which gives the fermented drink a funky flavour with fizz.

The alcohol in the presence of oxygen can get further broken down into acetic acid and water, giving vinegar. This is why open bottles of wine not consumed for a long time can turn into wine vinegar.

Yeast breaks down starches into basic sugars and then sugars into alcohol and carbon dioxide, which is how beer is made.

Playing with variables like a sealed lid versus a muslin-covered lid, sugar content in the starting solution and time taken for fermentation will lead to different results.

The more the sugar in the starting mixture, the more alcohol in your drink. You can restrict access to oxygen by storing the beverages in clip-top jars so the alcohol level is retained and is not converted into acid. Alcohol is volatile, which is why it will evaporate if kept in a breathable cloth-covered jar.

For a sourer ferment, give it more time and more oxygen (mesh or muslin cover for the jar). For a higher percentage of alcohol and carbonation, keep a sealed lid.

Lacto-fermented food like pickles, yoghurt or hot sauce can be refrigerated for a long shelf life. Fermented stuff like vinegar or hot sauces can also be pasteurized once they are ready, to make sure that they are shelf-stable, but this process kills all the live bacterial cultures in the fermented products.

Some examples of fermentation:
Grapes + yeast > alcoholic fermentation = wine
Fruit + yeast + acetic acid-bacteria = vinegar
Soybeans + aspergillus mould = tempeh

Let us take a closer look at the process in two very common fermentations.

Yoghurt

Lactobacteria are our everyday friends who help us convert milk to yoghurt. A small quantity of yoghurt (culture) is added to milk that has been heated and then cooled to lukewarm (around 45°C). The lactose in milk is fermented into lactic acid by the bacteria introduced via the culture. Lactic acid curdles the milk proteins to give yoghurt its creamy texture and tangy flavour. Chillies or ginger can also be used instead of a yoghurt culture to kickstart lacto-fermentation of milk as there are enough bacteria on the surface of ginger and stalks of chillies.

Lacto-fermented pickles

In the making of lacto-fermented vegetables (pickles), lactic acid bacteria along with some yeasts break down sugars to get lactic acid and alcohol. The acidic environment with low or no oxygen, along with salt, helps create an environment that is suitable to grow good bacteria and unsuitable for harmful organisms like fungi and mould. In the presence of oxygen or if part of the vegetable or fruit you want to lacto-ferment is not submerged in brine, it will most likely catch some unwanted microorganisms that will cause mould.

Basic Equipment Needed for Fermentation

Kitchen scales: Most lacto-fermentation projects use brine, and the quantity of salt must be precisely calculated so that the salt level is just right to keep the bad bacteria away and not so much as to hamper fermentation. Buy digital scales but without a bowl attachment so you can use any kind of jar to weigh. Scales are also very useful in baking and soap-making.

Glass jars with lids: Glass is the best material for fermenting jars. It is easy to sterilize or clean and gives good visibility of the contents that are fermenting. It is reasonably inexpensive compared to ceramic or fermentation-grade steel. Metals can get corroded during the fermentation process and impart a metallic flavour to the food or beverage.

Once you start fermenting, you will automatically start hoarding glass jars. If you care about having a neat and aesthetic look for your fermentation station, buy sets of jars of 500 ml, 1 litre and 2 litres. If you are just starting off, use what you have or borrow from neighbours and friends. You can also source them from your neighbourhood restaurants or bars that may have larger-sized glass jars in which they buy certain ingredients like olives or pickled jalapeños.

Wooden chopsticks: Useful to stir tall bottles or jars.

Pieces of cotton cloth or kitchen paper along with rubber bands: Needed to close the mouth of the jar in case you want some oxygen to enter the bottle— as in the making of kombucha—while preventing any insects from entering.

Clip-top jars and bottles: These are useful for building carbonation in fizzy drinks such as the second fermentation of whey sodas, ginger ales and kombuchas. Do follow the safety instructions given below while using clip-top bottles.

Labels: Once you get into a fermentation frenzy, it is easy to lose track of what is in which bottle and your fridge shelves will have a crowd of condiments in nameless bottles. An easy way to label is to use masking tape and a marker pen. Write the name, ingredients and date. It is good to remember the ingredients that went in, in case you want to be careful when gifting it to friends who may have allergies.

All the equipment used for fermentation needs to be washed well with hot water and soap. All traces of soap should be washed thoroughly and the equipment air- or sun-dried. There should be no microbes in the jar or introduced via used dishcloths, etc. It could throw the microbial balance in the ferment out of whack.

Safety Precautions

Carbon dioxide is released during the process of fermentation. When a fermented beverage is kept in a sealed bottle, pressure can build up in the bottle, making it eventually explode. If you use a corked bottle, you can see how the pressure in the bottle blows off the cork.

Refrigeration slows down the process considerably. Half a day at room temperature is almost equal to a week or two in the refrigerator. It is important to 'burp' bottles left at room temperature once or twice a day, depending on how hot it is where you live. The hotter the temperature, the faster the fermentation. Burping is nothing but very gradually opening the lid to let out the pressure and sealing it again.

The other safety precaution is to be wary of unfriendly microorganisms. Visual and olfactory cues are your best guides to tell you if the fermented product is safe or not. Black or grey mould-like substances and a foul odour are definite reasons to discard your ferment.

On Home-Fermented Beverages

All home-fermented drinks at room temperature can be served along with a meal. They are much better than commercial drinks, which come with excessive sugar, and they have the added benefit of gut-beneficial bacteria.

Some readymade commercial drinks are called 'beer' and 'ale' like ginger ale, but these are purely chemical-based carbonated drinks with no trace of fermentation as their misleading names suggest.

The trend of kombucha, fermented ginger beer and kefir is here to stay. These cost a bomb when bought and they are so easy to make at home, so why not try these out? You don't need any fancy ingredients or equipment. Beverages are one of the easiest fermentation experiments to get started with. They are also quicker compared to some of the other slower ferments. While some beverages like kombucha take time, many other fermented beverages are ready in just two to three days.

Fermented beverages can be classified into three kinds:

1. Require a SCOBY (symbiotic culture of bacteria and yeast)
2. Require other starters like ginger bug and whey
3. Wild ferments

Drinks like kombucha and water kefir require a SCOBY to get started. Ginger ales and whey sodas need a ginger bug and whey respectively to inoculate the starter cultures. Wild ferments such as tepache harness bacteria on the surface of pineapple peels and core.

The base liquid to prepare a fermented drink is a mixture of water and sugar. Some of the water can be replaced by a fruit juice, herbal infusion or black tea. The sugar can be replaced by mashed fruits, jaggery, honey or any other sugar source. The initial culture could come from yoghurt whey, milk kefir whey, ginger bug, plain kombucha, SCOBY, water kefir crystals, sprouted grains or yoghurt.

Examples of home-made fermented beverages are ginger ale, beet kvass, water kefir, kombucha, whey sodas and tepache.

> **Some Common Kitchen Ingredients You Can Ferment**
>
> Milk: yoghurt, milk kefir
> Garlic: lacto-fermented garlic, salsa
> Onions: lacto-fermented onions, hot sauce, salsa
> Tomato: salsa, lacto-fermented tomato chutneys
> Herbs: salsa, whey sodas, fermented pulps
> Honey: honey-fermented garlic, lemon honey ferment
> Chillies: hot sauce, chillies in brine
> Beets: lacto-fermented beets, kanji, kvass (beet sour)
> Carrots: lacto-fermented carrots, kanji
> Mustard seeds: used in hot sauce, lacto-fermented pickles, kanji
> Cabbage: kimchi, sauerkraut
> Apples: in hot sauce, apple-spices-sugar ferment, whey soda
> Pineapple: tepache, hot sauce, whey soda

Some Common Fermented Foods from India and Around the World

Different parts of India have been into fermenting different foods depending on the geography, ethnicity, climate conditions and cultural practices in that zone. The fermented foods in India can be broadly divided based on the raw materials used.[7]

Plant-based: (1) fermented cereal foods; (2) fermented non-soybean legume foods; (3) fermented soybean foods; and (4) fermented vegetable foods

Animal-based: (1) fermented dairy foods; (2) fermented/sun-dried/smoked fish products; and (3) fermented/sun-dried/smoked meat products

Alcoholic beverages: (1) amylolytic starters for production of alcoholic beverages and (2) alcoholic beverages

Others: fermented tea, crabs, fruit

Fermented rice-legume batters are found in south Indian cuisine.

Fermented legume (non-soybean) based foods are common in north, west and central India.

Fermented soybeans and vegetables are found in all the North-eastern states.

Fermented dairy is seen in all of India except the North-east.

Fermented alcoholic beverages are also seen almost all over India.

---

[7] Source: *International Journal of Current Microbiology and Applied Sciences*, 7, 4(2018) 1873–83, Traditional Fermented Products of India

Some Fermented Foods from India

Cereal/ legume-based	Legume-based	Dairy-based	Vegetable-based	Alcoholic
	Dhokla	Dahi	Gundruk (green leafy vegetable)	Angoori
Idli	Adai	Chaas	Ekung (young bamboo shoots)	Ark
Dosa	Dhuska bari	Chhurpi	Inziang-dui (mustard leaves)	Basi
Appam	Kanji vada	Kadhi		Chhang
Adhirasam	Papad	Dahi vada		Feni
Bhatura	Khaman			Mahua
Bhabhru	Akhonii			Madhu
Chzot	Kinema			Neera
Curd rice/ panta bhath				Toddy/ Kallu
Dhuka				
Enduri Pitha				
Handwo				
Jalebi				
Koozh				
Sannas				
Selroti				

Fermentation Around the World:

Africa: fermented grain porridges
Europe: fermented dairy, cultured butter, sauerkraut, herbs, cider
Alaska: fermented fish
Asia: pickled vegetables, kimchi, sauces

Resources:

Happy Live Cultures for water kefir grains, milk kefir grains and kombucha SCOBY (https://www.happylivecultures.in/)
Sattvic Foods for kombucha SCOBY (sattvicfoods.in)
Heal Your Gut for water kefir grains and kombucha SCOBY (healyourgut.in)
Urban Platter brand water and milk kefir cultures (urbanplatter.in)

Interview with Payal Shah of Kobo Fermentary

Payal Shah is the founder of Kobo Fermentary. She is a shepherd of microbes and has been an avid fermenter for nearly two decades.

How did you get into fermentation?

My adventures with fermentation started a long time ago with my grandmother when I was five, and I was roped into projects that she was doing. I was subconsciously picking up the nuances around fermentation since those days, which I didn't even realize until I started my own journey when I was eighteen.

My journey into fermentation started with ginger ale, which I was obsessed with for three or four years when I was eighteen and in college. I had this ginger drink somewhere and kept thinking about that flavour, wanting to replicate it. I started researching this; my first few batches were not great, but I kept going and tweaking my method until I got it right. Home-made ginger ale tastes so much better than anything that's commercially available, that you can get hooked.

Broadly, what are the categories in fermentation?

From a science perspective, a lot of ferments are usually a combination of yeast and bacteria—we could classify these as ferments that use salt and those that use sugar, under which there is aerobic and anaerobic fermentation, and then dairy ferments that use neither salt nor sugar.

What do you suggest someone new to fermentation should start with? Please share a couple of beginner-friendly projects.

A beginner should start with something they like— for example, if you like fizzy drinks then start your experiments with that, and if someone likes sour pickles, then that's the place to start. Make something that you like to eat or drink. That will keep you interested and your journey going.

The following projects are low-effort, high-return and beginner-friendly.

A honey ferment with chillies, garlic or fruit just sitting in a jar of honey for two days to a week is a great place to start as there is no measuring or anything technical involved. You end up with something fragrant and delicious.

Whey soda in which whey collected from dairy yoghurt or vegan yoghurt or kefir is used to inoculate any fruit juice, ginger juice or lime juice gives a fizzy, refreshing drink.

Does one need a lot of time investment in these projects?

Fermentation is a lesson in patience. Many of the projects take time. I'd also like to point out to anyone who is just getting started with this journey that the time is not your time. You are just waiting around for the microbes to do their work. It's just five to ten minutes of your active time at one go. So you don't need much of a personal time investment.

What is some of the equipment that is good to have to conduct these fermentation experiments?

People have been fermenting for thousands of years before any equipment was available. While it is a lot of science, it is totally doable with things around your kitchen. All kinds of glass jars and bottles are good, a minimum size would be 200 ml to 1- to 2-litre jars for fizzy drinks and kombucha, etc. Anything in this range will work fine.

In terms of ingredients, you can ferment most of the foods you eat and these are easily found in the kitchen or the vegetable shop.

Sieves, spoons, chopsticks, paper towels or cloths to tie around the neck of the jars are some of the other things required.

What kind of materials are best to use for fermentation?

Glass is used as it is cheap, easily replaced and easily available, and easy to sterilize. The downside is that it can break. Steel can corrode as it reacts with acidity.

In the timeline of fermentation, plastic is a very new material. We don't know if the fermented matter will react with plastic to release any unwanted chemicals. Also, the surface of plastic could have micro-abrasions where the microbes could lodge and colonize, so it is tough to sterilize as well as you can glass.

Ceramics have been used for fermentation for a very long time in many cultures. One should be sure that the glaze is not lead-based, which can react with acidity to release poisonous substances.

When it comes to fermentation, should we follow our instincts or follow instructions to a T?

My own foray into fermentation started off with following my instincts, but the science has made my understanding more concrete. Both instinct and science go hand-in-hand in fermentation. With science-backed knowledge, the process can be carried out with more resolve. Using weighing scales or backing up your instincts with science will help you succeed more often.

Could you share a few tips on how to convert a fermentation hobby into a business?

I had a physical fermentary where I was producing fermented stuff for two and a half years. I just closed it down before the pandemic.

Fermentation done at home is very different from commercial fermentation. As complicated as it is doing it in the kitchen for yourself, it is much more complex when done at a commercial level, because you are managing that many different microbes, without wastage, and achieving consistency.

At home, it is okay if one batch of ferment turns out different from the previous one, but at a commercial level, consistency is important. Microbes behave differently at a commercial level, and it is difficult to control. You are also aiming for a middle ground where your product appeals to a wider audience.

Health and safety issues like FSSAI certification and understanding the scale of things is a different challenge altogether. Other things to consider are use of space, equipment and ensuring that all of the stuff is shelf-stable.

But it is not impossible for someone who is really passionate about it to get into a fermentation business. You need to take care of the business side of things like logistics and marketing. Fermenting may take up 25 per cent of your time and 75 per cent will be spent on business, operations and logistics.

There are so many different avenues in this space as the ferments are never-ending. You can also create new stuff. The creative side of this is incredibly fulfilling.

Producing kombucha, pickles, koji and the other Japanese technologies of fermentation, blending many of these techniques together—there is a lot of scope for different products if you are able to scale it and build it into a commercial business.

Sharing knowledge on this subject or teaching is another business avenue. You can teach individuals, train personnel in cafés and restaurants on fermentation techniques, and offer expert consultancy to brands in this space.

Is there a surge of interest in this space in the current times?

Internationally, the fermentation space has blown up in the last couple of years. There is a surge of interest in the subject. If you go to a café or restaurant, kombucha is on the menu, and people also want to make it themselves at home. There's a lot of research happening on the microbial world, and this revivalist movement is only going to gather more momentum.

Projects

1. Rejuvelac/Probiotic Water   145
2. Vegan Cheese   146
3. Whey Lemon Soda and Other Whey Sodas   147
4. Kanji: A Ferment from North India   149
5. Ginger Bug and Ginger Ale   151
6. Tepache   152
7. Lacto-fermented Mustard Condiment   154
8. Lacto-fermented Salsa   156
9. Lacto-fermented Hot Sauce   157
10. Mango Vinegar   159

Chocolate cake

Chocolate chip cookies

Basic loaf of bread

Sourdough starter

Sourdough waffles

Molaga podi

Paruppu podi

Salted caramel
sauce with a
splash of rum

Ginger ale,
turmeric bug
and ginger bug

Tepache

Lacto-fermented
hot sauce in the
making

Lacto-fermented
hot sauce and
brine

Green goddess hair oil

Sheer botanical soap

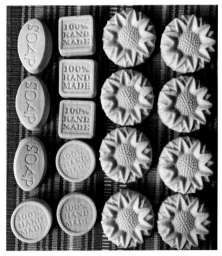

Castile soap

Dishwashing soap

Soap coloured
with avocado tea

Melt-and-pour soap

Mustard microgreens

Growing tomatoes

Tea-dyed tea towel

Reusable bowl covers

Crochet hair scrunchies

Crochet hot pads

1. Rejuvelac/Probiotic Water

This is the easiest fermentation project to get started off with. All you need is one ingredient—grains of wheat. Water fermented with sprouted wheat grains gives this drink a pleasant lemony flavour that you will be happy to sip on every day. Rejuvelac is rich in strains of lactobacilli.

Gather

2-litre glass jar
Small square of cloth + rubber band
1 cup wholewheat grains
Water

Make

Soak the wholewheat grains in a litre of water for twelve hours. Drain the water after twelve hours.

Using any preferred sprouting method, keep these grains to sprout until the sprouts are longer than the grain itself. At this point, you can either rinse the sprouts one last time or skip the rinsing.

Place the sprouts in a 1-litre jar and fill it up with drinking water, leaving around 1 inch of headspace. Cover this with a cotton cloth or a piece of kitchen paper, securing it with a rubber band.

The fermentation time depends upon the weather. Hot, humid weather conditions are favourable to fermentation. Keep the jar in a warm place.

Taste the rejuvelac after twenty-four hours. If it tastes like water, then ferment for another twenty-four hours. You're looking for a slight beer-like aroma with a pleasant lemony tang. If you get a foul odour, it means that unwanted, bad bacteria have gate-crashed the rejuvelac party. You should discard the batch and start over.

When the rejuvelac is ready, strain and drink or decant into bottles and refrigerate. The same sprouts can be used to make two more batches. The subsequent batches will take a shorter time to ferment.

Once you have mastered this process, you can make a similar probiotic water with grains like quinoa and finger millet.

2. Vegan Cheese

Once you have made rejuvelac, the next obvious step is to make your own cheese. Let me tell you that you don't have to be vegan to enjoy this cheese. I love a variety of dairy cheeses, but the joy in making your own cheese (from scratch) is pretty darn fulfilling. Imagine telling your friends that you handmade the cheeses adorning the cheese board?

Gather

500 ml glass jar
Small square of cloth + rubber band
1 cup cashew nuts (broken is fine)
1 tsp mustard seeds (yellow is preferable)
⅓ cup rejuvelac

Make

Soak the cashews and mustard seeds in warm water for two hours. Drain and add to a mixer jar with the rejuvelac and blend to get a somewhat coarse paste.

Scoop out the paste into a glass jar. Cover the jar with a piece of kitchen paper or a cloth and secure it with a rubber band.

Depending on the room temperature, the fermentation process should take anywhere between twelve to twenty-four hours. The cheese mass will float on the top of mostly clear liquid, which is whey.

Gently separate the cheese solids using a spoon and place it in a square of muslin cloth or cheesecloth. Bring the ends together and keep in a sieve over a bowl to collect the excess moisture/whey. This should take around thirty minutes. The cheese is now ready for use. If not eating it right away, keep it in an airtight container in the fridge and use it within two days. It can also be wrapped in a beeswax wrap and stored in the refrigerator.

The whey in the process of making this vegan cheese can be kept in a jar in the fridge for use in other fermentation projects like whey soda.

3. Whey Lemon Soda and Other Whey Sodas

Think of this like the sweet lime soda you order in a restaurant but naturally fermented. It is one of the easiest fermented drinks to make, refreshing in hot weather and a good digestive when having a meal.

It is easy to make your own whey from home-made yoghurt. Line a sieve with a muslin cloth and place

around 600 to 700 g of yoghurt in the sieve. Bring
the ends of the cloth together and secure them with
a rubber band. Place the sieve over a bowl. In one to
two hours, you'll have enough whey collected to make
your own whey lemonade. The sugar initially added
to the mixture is mostly used up during fermentation,
so if the lemonade is not sweet enough for your taste,
you can sweeten it with some more sugar after the
fermentation process.

Gather

2-litre glass jar
Small square of cloth + rubber band
⅓ cup sugar
1200 ml water
⅓–½ cup lime juice
⅓ cup whey
4 × 500 ml flip-top bottles

Make

Add the sugar and water to the glass jar and stir until
the sugar is nearly dissolved.

Mix in the lime juice and whey. Stir well.

Cover the mouth of the jar with a muslin cloth
secured with a string or a rubber band. Keep aside for
two days. This depends on the weather (hotter weather
leads to faster fermentation) and how you want it to
taste. You should see some bubbles, and when you taste
the drink it will have a more complex flavour than just
plain lemonade.

Once the taste is to your liking, for the second fermentation (F2), decant the whey soda into flip-top bottles leaving 1 to 2 inches of headspace in each. Refrigerate it to develop more fizz. Be careful to burp the bottle if you don't drink it in two or three days as excess pressure may build up in the bottles, leading to explosions.

Once you have tried this basic lemon whey soda, you can make endless varieties using other fruits and their scraps such as plums, mangoes, berries, grapes, etc., or even vegetables like beets.

My other favourite whey soda is whey + water + ¼ cup beet juice (squeeze 1 grated beet) + 5–6 slices ginger. After two days or so of fermentation, pass the soda through a sieve before bottling it.

Notes: Reserve some whey soda from the previous batch to add to the next batch as an inoculum. This can be used instead of whey itself.

If you make milk kefir, the whey from the kefir can also be used to make whey sodas.

4. Kanji: A Ferment from North India

The first time I had kanji was at my Marwari friend's home. The dish was kanji vada where deep fried vadas made of urad dal batter were dipped in a thin mustard seed-fermented liquid. It was something I hadn't tasted before, and I loved the unique flavour of it. The kanji is made three or four days in advance of the day it is planned to be served, so that the optimum level of fermentation is reached.

Another kanji made during springtime, especially Holi, is with black or purple carrots available during this time of the year in north India. The pungent flavour of mustard seeds makes this a unique savoury drink to celebrate the change of seasons.

Gather

2-litre glass jar
Small square of cloth + rubber band
4 tsp mustard seeds (yellow or brown or a combination of both)
3 carrots
1 beet
1-½ litres water
1 tbsp rock salt

Make

Grind the mustard seeds to a coarse powder either in a spice grinder or using a mortar and pestle.

Peel and cut the carrots and beet into batons.

In a large glass jar, combine the mustard powder, vegetables, water and salt. Give it a good stir.

The vegetables should be immersed well.

Cover with a muslin cloth secured with a rubber band around the neck. Keep the jar out in a sunny spot in the daytime, bringing it inside for the night.

Give it a stir every day. The process can take anywhere from four to seven days depending on the weather conditions. Fermentation is faster in hot weather.

Close the jar with a lid and refrigerate. Serve chillies with the vegetable pieces on the side.

5. Ginger Bug and Ginger Ale

This is your handy-dandy starter that will help you make many fermented drinks, starting with the very popular ginger ale. Use organic ginger as far as possible as you want to use it with the peel because organic ginger tends to not be irradiated. Irradiation kills off a lot of the natural microorganisms that help with the fermentation. Try a mix of fresh ginger, turmeric and galangal for a complex flavour profile. It takes under a week to get going. Once you have this starter handy, it's your gateway to many delicious, fermented drinks. The skin of ginger, as in the case of all root vegetables, is a rich source of lactobacillus and wild yeast.

Gather

400 ml glass jar
Small square of cloth + rubber band
1 tbsp grated fresh ginger with peel (or 2 tbsp chopped ginger)
1 tbsp sugar
1-½ cups filtered water

For every feed:
1 tbsp grated ginger (or 2 tbsp chopped)
1 tbsp sugar
2 tbsp filtered water

Make

Take a clean glass bottle and fill it with the starting ingredients of ginger, sugar and filtered water. Seal with a lid. Once a day, feed it with the ingredients listed under 'feed' for three to five days or until you see that the mixture is foamy and bubbly, which means that the ginger bug is ready.

To use the ginger bug, strain the bug to get half a cup of clear liquid. Combine with seven and a half cups of prepared lemonade or green tea or ginger-lemongrass brew, and pour into a large jar. Cover with a cloth and a rubber band and keep on the counter for five to six days or until you see some bubbles and it tastes fermented.

Remove this to flip-top bottles and refrigerate. Burp the bottles every two days (open the lid gently and let the gas escape) or else the pressure can build up and make the bottles burst.

Tip: Chop or grate all the required ginger on day one and keep it in a container in the fridge so you don't have to do this before each feed.

6. Tepache

If you buy a pineapple weighing 750 g, nearly 300 to 350 g of it comprising the crown, the peel and the core ends up becoming food waste. Tepache is an amazing way to convert inedible pineapple scraps into a delicious drink. It is also one of the easiest fruit to make fermented drinks with that is ready in just two to three days. Kickstart your fermentation journey with tepache and you will be hooked to its simplicity and flavour.

Choose an organic pineapple if possible. Wash and scrub the ripe pineapple with a vegetable brush or a new toothbrush to remove any soil from the surface. Do not wash it with soap as you need the wild yeast on the surface of the fruit to enable the process of fermentation.

Tepache is a traditional drink from Mexico, which used to be prepared from corn. The name has a Nahuatl origin, 'tepatti' meaning 'maize drink'. The local sweetener 'piloncillo', which looks somewhat like dark jaggery, is used along with the pineapple peels and spices to make the drink. You can use raw cane sugar or powdered jaggery instead. Cinnamon and cloves are the spices used traditionally.

Gather

2-litre glass jar
Small square of cloth + rubber band
Peel and core of 1 ripe pineapple
2 cinnamon sticks
4–5 cloves
¾ cup sugar or powdered jaggery
1 litre water

Make

Combine all the ingredients in a glass jar. Stir well.

Cover with a square of cloth or kitchen paper secured with a rubber band. The liquid should be aerated for the aerobic fermentation process so do not cover with an airtight lid.

In twelve to twenty-four hours, depending on the climate conditions, you should start seeing some bubbles in the jar. If you see white scum on the surface, skim it off. Give the liquid a stir and cover the jar once again with a tissue or cheesecloth.

Stir the jar every twelve hours and taste the tepache. In two to three days, the tepache will be ready. Taste the tepache every day and stop the fermentation process when the flavour is to your liking.

Once the tepache is ready, strain the liquid and refrigerate or serve immediately over ice cubes.

Notes: While storing a pineapple, store it crown side down for proper ripening. When stored upright, gravity forces all the sugars to concentrate at the base, making the bottom ripen faster than the top, and rotting before the whole fruit ripens. Like all tropical fruits, the best way to tell if it is well ripened is to smell the base of the fruit. If you get a sweet pineapple aroma, then the fruit is ready to be cut.

7. Lacto-fermented Mustard Condiment

The pungent flavour of mustard makes any dish pop. This paste is inspired by the Bengali tomato kashundi. Use tart desi tomatoes if possible although, when in season, raw mangoes make a great substitute for tomatoes.

Fermentation adds another layer of depth to this mustard condiment. While you can make a small bottle, it does make sense to make a larger quantity given that it takes two weeks to get ready. You can always give it to friends and family.

Gather

1-litre glass jar with lid
½ cup yellow mustard seeds
2 tbsp black mustard seeds
5 medium-sized ripe tomatoes, roughly chopped
5–6 green chillies, sliced
10 cloves garlic, roughly chopped
1 tbsp chopped fresh turmeric (or use 1 tsp ground turmeric)
Salt (to be calculated)

Make

Soak the mustard seeds in water for two hours.

Drain and combine with all the other ingredients except salt in a blender to get a coarse paste.

Place a bowl on a kitchen scale. Tare the scale to zero before adding the contents of the blender into the bowl. Add some water if the paste is too thick.

Note the weight. Calculate the salt for the recipe at 4 per cent of the total weight of the other ingredients. Combine the measure of salt into the mustard mixture in the bowl and stir well.

Transfer this into a glass jar with a lid and ferment for ten to fifteen days. Refrigerate the jars of the condiment when fermentation is complete.

Use over hard-boiled eggs, in salad dressings or instead of ketchup along with fries or other snacks.

Notes: You can make your own honey mustard sauce by combining ¼ cup of this fermented mustard paste along with 2 tbsp each of honey and vinegar.

8. Lacto-fermented Salsa

This is tastier than regular salsa with a complex flavour. Add it to salads, mix it into mayo or serve it as is with chips. The brine that gets formed in the jar is flavour gold too. Add it to cocktails or bread dough or any dish you want to give a kick of flavour.

Gather

2 × 1-litre glass jars with lids
7–8 ripe medium-sized tomatoes
1 medium-sized onion
10–12 garlic cloves
7–8 green chillies (or jalapeños)
¼ cup chopped coriander with stems
4 tbsp lime juice
Coarsely powdered rock salt (to be calculated)

Make

Chop the tomatoes and onions roughly. Transfer to a food processor and pulse a few times until you get a coarse chunky puree.

Keep a large bowl on a weighing scale. Tare the scale to zero and transfer the onion-tomato mix along with all the other ingredients to the bowl. Note the weight of the ingredients. Take 3 per cent of the total weight in salt. Mix in the salt.

Divide the salsa between two clean, dry 1-litre jars making sure there is enough room on the top. Close tightly with lids and keep undisturbed away from direct sunlight for two to four days. The lacto-fermented salsa is ready.

Keep this in the fridge with labels and date. It will stay for over six months in the fridge.

9. Lacto-fermented Hot Sauce

Once you start making these lacto-fermented hot sauces at home, you will never want to buy another bottle. With each season, you can add your own twists to the taste—mangoes in summer, fresh turmeric in winter, apples when they come in season and so on. Make sure to use a mix of chilli varieties, a fruity element and a few aromatic elements to have a complex flavoured sauce. The vinegary sourness of supermarket hot sauces is not a patch on the rich, deep flavour of these lacto-fermented hot sauces. You don't need me to tell you the number of ways you can enjoy a good hot sauce!

Gather

2-litre glass jar with lid
3 cups of mixed fresh chillies (green, red)
¼ cup peeled garlic cloves
1–2 apples
2–3 amlas (Indian gooseberries), chopped (optional)
¼ cup chopped coriander stems
1 tbsp black mustard seeds
Salt
2–3 cabbage leaves

Make

Slice off the stems of the chillies and chop roughly.

Wash apples well and chop roughly.

Place the jar on the kitchen scale and tare to zero.

Add the chillies, garlic, apples, coriander stems and mustard seeds. Press down with a spatula.

Pour enough clean drinking water into the jar to submerge all the ingredients. Check the total weight of the contents of the jar (don't include jar weight).

Weigh 3 per cent of the total weight in salt. For example, if ingredients plus water weight is 1000 g, then you will need 30 g of salt. Use any kind of salt. Add the salt to the jar and give it a good stir with a chopstick or a wooden ladle.

Place a couple of cabbage leaves on the surface of the mixture to ensure that the other ingredients remain submerged in brine. Any exposed ingredient can catch mould.

Cover this with a tight-fitting lid. Keep this aside in a cool, dry place for three weeks.

After the chillies and other ingredients have lacto-fermented for three weeks, pass it through a sieve. Place the solids in a blender and blend to a smooth puree, adding some of the brine to adjust the consistency. You can add some more salt, sugar or vinegar as per your requirement to balance the flavours before bottling the hot sauce. Keep it refrigerated. The flavours will develop further as the sauce slowly ferments in the fridge.

10. Mango Vinegar

Making your own fruit vinegar takes care of all the fruit waste and any imperfect produce. It also allows you to enjoy the flavour of the seasonal fruits available for a short period in the year for a long duration, albeit in another form. Mango vinegar can be used in salad dressings, as a souring agent in curries in place of tamarind and to add a kick to drinks. Organic fruit is best for use in these fermentation products as the skin of the fruit carries a lot of natural yeast that helps in the process of fermenting.

Makes around 700 ml.

Gather

2-litre glass jar with lid
Small square of cloth + rubber band

Peels and stone of 4–5 mangoes*
⅓ cup raw sugar (e.g. khandsari)
600–700 ml water
¼ cup raw vinegar** (starter)

Make

In a clean dry glass jar, add the peels and stones of the mangoes, sugar, water and raw vinegar. Stir well until sugar dissolves.

Cover with two layers of muslin cloth or cheesecloth and secure with a string or rubber band. This keeps the mixture aerated while keeping any insects out. Oxygen is required for this phase of fermentation.

Give this a stir once a day for one week and secure the cloth back. Stir it once every two to three days during week two.

After two weeks, filter out the solids and pour the liquid back into a jar and close with a plastic lid. Keep on the kitchen shelf for four to five weeks for this to turn into mango vinegar. You may find a thin, membrane-like layer forming and floating on the top. This is called the mother, which is a cloud of bacteria, yeast, protein and enzymes. You can use this along with some of the vinegar to make another batch.

---

* Some flesh sticking to the stone and peels is fine.
** Use home-made raw vinegar or use a store-bought natural vinegar that specifies 'with mother'.
Try the same recipe using any other fruit peels, seeds and/or core such as plums, pineapples and cherries.

Chapter 5

Home-Made Beauty

'Self-care starts with skincare.'

—Anon

As a kid, I would find advertisements for shampoos in bright pinks, yellows and blues fascinating. I started using commercial shampoos, that too sparingly, in my late teens. Until then, it was only grandma-approved *shikakai* and *reetha* powder mixed in water that was used as a 'shampoo' after the weekly hair and body oil massage.

All I need to do is close my eyes and I am transported to the balcony with the grills of our Mumbai home, which was the designated spot for oil massages. I remember the aroma of the oil warmed up with spices like black peppercorns and ginger slices and the feeling of hot oil slowly getting absorbed into my scalp, aided by the steady drumming of my grandfather's fingers.

I didn't appreciate it much then. Having to get my head doused in oil, the smell of which was too strong, and then wait around with an oily head for an hour or so followed by the hair wash—it was never fun. The hair-wash slurry would invariably get into my eyes, making them smart and water, the culprit being reetha or soap nuts. The silver lining was a good lunch to appease the massage and bath-induced hunger pangs. The ensuing nap was nothing short of bliss.

My maternal grandmother had a glowing face right up to her last days in her late eighties. The secret was *kasturi manjal*, also known as Cucurma aromatica or wild turmeric. This is different from the turmeric used for culinary purposes. It has a strong aroma and is used for skincare and beauty. After a bath, the dried knob of turmeric was rubbed on the wet stone and a smidgen of the fresh paste applied on the face, especially around the sideburns. This was to keep the sideburn hair from growing and to keep the face glowing. One can spin a patriarchal angle here, but I see it as women taking care of themselves with naturally available ingredients that were good for them.

Adulting is realizing what a luxury it was growing up with grandparents who did their best to instil the rituals of taking care of yourself and taught you to value natural hair and skincare over everything else. If I remember right, a lot of my friends would use the newest shampoo brands available in the market, if not buying the whole bottle, then the single-use sachets, which were available for one rupee or so (for those of you trying to do the math, it was the early to mid-1980s!). That made me feel deprived of the fun of using products that seemed to look and smell so much better than shikakai. As a girl growing up, I hated having the yellow hue of kasturi manjal on my face, and I would run away from the sight of it. Current life update: As the circle of life dictates, I have both the hair-wash powder and kasturi manjal in my bathroom cabinet today, and my grandmother is no doubt smiling-smirking at me from heaven.

Over the last decade or so, I have found joy in using home-made and all-natural products for skin and hair. Having access to a garden and growing useful herbs like curry leaves, hibiscus, moringa, betel leaf, henna, etc., makes the process even more fulfilling. While I love making soaps and shampoo bars from scratch, the herbal ingredients, each with their own benefit, make for excellent beauty, skin and haircare products. Also, it is far easier to blend them together in small quantities as per the condition of the skin and hair at the moment. I have shared many of these home-made DIY skin and hair remedies on my blog and social media over the years, and I would love for you to try out these 'recipes'.

Benefits of Making Skin and Haircare Products

1. No one knows your skin and hair the way you do. The condition of one's skin and hair varies with the seasons, hormones, diet, stress levels and so on. With the knowledge and the habit of creating beauty remedies at home, one can customize these products as per personal requirements.

2. When you make these products at home, you can use the best quality ingredients with no added colours, chemicals or preservatives. Ever wondered why a shampoo needs to be red or blue in colour to appeal to customers, or why it needs to have the artificial fragrance of strawberries or mangoes? When made at home, you can avoid all the unnecessary elements and focus only on what's beneficial. Products can be made without nasty ingredients like sodium lauryl sulphate (SLS) and parabens.

3. We all have an apothecary in our kitchen, or in our neighbourhood store. Herbs and roots in the tropical part of the world are naturally fragrant as they compete with each other for insect pollination. The experience of making and using these products is in itself aromatherapy.

4. What better self-care than understanding the needs of your hair and skin and formulating a combination of herbs and ingredients to suit that need? The whole process of coming up with a recipe, making it and bottling it is a source of mindful joy and fulfilment. And, of course, there is the satisfaction of using something created by yourself for pampering your skin and hair with the purest and best of ingredients.

5. Branded products often invest a lot in design and packaging. It is not only important for the brand image but also to ensure that the products aren't damaged in transit. When you make these products at home on a smaller scale for yourself, for family and gifting purposes,

they can be packaged in more eco-friendly ways using paper and recycled glass bottles. This reduces the usage of plastic.

6. Handmade beauty products make for the most thoughtful and cherished gifts for family and friends. They also make practical sense. When we buy 250 g each of six or seven ingredients and put them together, it amounts to over 1.5 kg, which is quite a lot to use up all by ourselves.

7. Homemade products for skin and hair are mostly vegan and do not involve animal testing.

8. This pursuit also saves you money on buying expensive hair and skin products.

9. Last but not least, with a growing market for all-natural products and self-care, if you are willing to put the effort into research and testing, it could grow into a good business.

Myths around Natural Products

All-natural does not mean 100 per cent chemical-free. Natural products like herbs are rich in phytochemicals, the therapeutic properties of which we seek to harness in the products.

All products do not suit all skin and hair types. Make small quantities and use them before deciding what works for your skin and hair.

There could also be allergic reactions to ingredients you are using for the first time. Always start with a patch test of individual ingredients that you have not used before. When gifting these products, always write down all the ingredients used, no matter how minuscule in quantity.

All-natural is not always cheaper than buying branded products. Buying several good-quality ingredients to prepare one product does add up. Pure essential oils are quite expensive too. Not all herbal products are gentle

---

What NOT to Put on Your Face

While we are talking about DIY skincare, there is one important thing to note. People tend to assume that anything from the kitchen is natural and therefore mild enough to put on your face. This is not true. Facial skin is very delicate compared to the skin on the rest of our body. More caution and care need to be exercised when trying out something for the face. Here are some of the ingredients you should not apply on your face and not use in home-made formulations.

1. **Lemon or lime juice** is citric acid with a pH of 2 and the pH of our skin is 4 to 5.5. The strong acid in lemon juice can burn the skin and cause hyperpigmentation.
2. **Vaseline** disturbs the delicate balance of bacteria and fungi on the skin (yes, skin has its own microbiome). It cuts out the oxygen and leads to acne as the bacteria multiply under the cover.
3. **Baking soda** with a pH of roughly 8, shifts the pH of the skin, which is naturally mildly acidic. Imbalance in skin causes a change in the microbiome, leading to flare-ups.

on skin and hair. Read up on the ingredients before using them in formulations.

Just because something is natural does not automatically make it better or more effective than a chemical formulation. Some natural ingredients do work while the efficacy of some is more of an urban legend.

Now that we have looked at what not to use in skincare formulations, let's peek into the skincare pantry where there are hundreds of natural ingredients stacked up, waiting to be picked up for your formulation.

Skincare Pantry

Here are some easily available ingredients that your skin will love, each with its own benefits. You can pick and choose from this list depending on the skin conditions you want to address in your home-made skincare product.

Aloe vera	Anti-inflammatory; heals sunburns, burns and wounds; soothes irritation from insect bites
Coconut oil	Antibacterial, antiviral, anti-inflammatory, excellent for dry skin
Turmeric	Anti-inflammatory, antibacterial, antioxidant, reduces sun damage, reduces acne, heals wounds and burns

Neem	Treatment of acne and skin infections, soothes irritated skin, helps deal with blackheads and whiteheads, anti-ageing, helps dry skin, improves radiance
Manjistha	Anti-inflammatory, antibacterial, antioxidant, improves complexion, reduces pigmentation
Tulsi	Antibacterial, antifungal, toner, cleanser, treats acne, anti-ageing, brightens complexion
Milk	A good cleanser, toner for dry skin, mild exfoliant, hydrates the skin, reduces pigmentation, lactic acid in milk helps lighten scars when used regularly
Cream	Moisturizes dry skin, brightens skin, improves skin tone and elasticity, lactic acid helps lighten scars over time
Yoghurt	Soothes irritated skin and sunburn, lightens pigmentation, moisturizes dry skin

Honey	Antibacterial, antiseptic, humectant (helps keep skin moist), moisturizing, gentle exfoliant, lightens scars when used over time, anti-ageing
Multani mitti	Exfoliant, tightens the skin, good for oily skin, improves skin texture, reduces pigmentation, deep cleanser
Cocoa	Rich in flavonoids that reduce oxidative stress on the skin, anti-inflammatory, anti-ageing
Sandalwood	Cooling, reduces inflammation
Rose water	Cools and soothes irritated skin, toner, reduces redness, anti-ageing, hydrates skin
Flours (besan, green gram, masoor dal)	Cleansers, exfoliants, soothe irritated skin, control excess sebum production (good for oily skin), control acne, reduce tan, remove fine facial hair

Haircare Pantry

Here are some easily available ingredients that help with lustrous locks. Choose the ingredients for your formulations depending on the hair problems to address.

Amla	Strengthens roots, reduces premature greying, antioxidant, improves hair growth, prevents and treats dandruff, reduces hair fall
Bhringraj	Reduces hair fall, improves hair growth, gives lustre to hair, repairs damaged hair, reduces premature greying
Brahmi	Reduces hair loss, cleanser, treats dandruff, strengthens roots, promotes hair growth, reduces dryness and itchiness of scalp
Coconut oil	Nourishing properties, gets absorbed into the scalp quickly, reduces breakage, improves condition of damaged hair, reduces frizz, improves volume
Fenugreek seeds	Anti-inflammatory, antifungal, stimulates hair growth, reduces hair fall, controls itchy scalp, works as a good conditioner
Shikakai	Reduces scalp itch and inflammation, soothes the scalp, reduces dandruff, restores natural oils in hair, promotes hair growth, cleanser
Hibiscus	Reduces hair fall, stops premature greying, gives lustre to hair, treats dandruff, prevents split ends, good conditioner

Curry leaves	Antioxidant, nourishes scalp, antibacterial, antifungal, cleanser, strengthens hair follicles, reduces hair fall
Soap nuts	Natural shampoo with lather, adds volume and shine to hair, prevents hair fall, reduces frizz
Flaxseed oil	Reduces hair fall, stimulates hair growth, nourishing, reduces dryness of scalp, reduces frizz
Tulsi	Reduces scalp itchiness, improves hair growth, reduces hair loss
Neem	Conditioner, promotes hair growth, strengthens follicles, reduces dandruff, treats head lice, antifungal, antibacterial

Interview with Aarushi Singhal of Blend it Raw Apothecary

Aarushi started her blog on organic skincare in 2015, when she was just nineteen. At twenty-four, she is the founder and owner of two brands, Blend it Raw Apothecary and Blended Botanica. Her brand has served over 30,000 customers, 70 to 80 per cent of them being repeat customers. She is certified in organic skincare formulations and is based out of Delhi.

Tell us a little bit about yourself, Aarushi.

I have an Economics Honours degree, and I simultaneously started this skincare brand. I am currently working on natural products where I supply raw herbs, oils and ingredients sourced from across India to customers. I also teach people DIY simple skin and haircare products using these sourced ingredients as well as kitchen ingredients. I am also passionate about learning everything related to aromatherapy, herbalism and Ayurveda.

What was your first step into the world of natural beauty products?

It all started from the kitchen. My mother and grandmother would make basic *ubtans*, Ayurvedic hair oils and their signature hair mask. That was my introduction to organic and natural skincare. I wanted to share my family's home remedies for hair and skin with like-minded people online. My first formal introduction to skin and haircare happened when I started my blog and enrolled myself in Formula Botanica, an institute based in London, where they teach organic skincare formulations. During this course, I learnt to make all these formulas from scratch.

Did you have other interests and beauty was one of them or did you know this was 'the one' for you? How did you turn this into a business?

Beauty was never one of my interests. I was a studious, nerdy child and my life revolved around books. My only aim then was to get a good job in an MNC. After I left school, I enrolled myself in Economics Honours and failed in my first semester, which is when I felt the need to do something creative and started my beauty blog, *Glitter Naturally*. After my second year of blogging, I started getting a lot of queries on what products I used in my DIY remedies such as moringa and coconut oil. My DIY combinations were a bit unique as compared to the usual ones, for example, aloe vera with oat milk for a hair mask. That's how my blog started getting eyeballs.

I started sourcing good-quality products so that I could satisfy the queries of people who were keen to buy these from me. I started off by selling five products and they started doing very well, which is when I considered this as my full-time career.

I started my brand after informally selling via Instagram.

My parents were against turning my hobby into a business as they just wanted me to have a steady, well-paying job, as I am neither from a business background nor an affluent family. When my business took off well, that is when my family was satisfied that it was okay for me to pursue this line.

What are some of the lesser known, all-natural or botanical ingredients that we should be using for our regular skin or haircare?

From the kitchen ingredients, plant-based milks such as almond, coconut and oat milk are great for both hair and skin, making for a great hair mask. Leftover pulp can be used as a body scrub.

Take a handful of tulsi, moringa and curry leaves and aloe vera pulp. Blend to a slimy paste, apply as a hair mask and face mask. Leave it on for thirty minutes and wash off as usual.

Use hibiscus roselle of the hibiscus family, rich in vitamin C, AHA and BHA, as a face mask—it works as an anti-ageing remedy by reducing fine lines and pigmentation.

Can you share a few routines for natural beauty that we should incorporate in our lives?

Be regular with a face mask at least twice a week at night after cleansing your skin. Two unique rituals that I follow:

In the morning, brew tea with any botanicals like tulsi, rose or cardamom. Wash your face with this botanical face tea.

Use a bath powder instead of soaps or shower gels.

Who are your main clients in terms of age, location, etc.? Are they urban, semi-urban, millennials or older people?

Most of my customers are women in the age group of thirty to forty-five years. The younger folk are not much into my kind of products as they prefer ready-to-use, highly fragranced products. They don't have time for DIY mixes and prefer quick fixes.

High-ticket orders are almost always from the older age group who realize the value of good-quality natural ingredients and don't mind some DIY component.

Most of our audience is from south India, especially Tamil Nadu, Kerala and Karnataka.

For someone who has a farm or is interested in this idea of botanical and all-natural beauty products, what are the steps they need to take to make this into a business?

Establish an audience, start talking about your farm, your farming techniques, what products you are using on your farm. If one botanical has multiple uses, figure out the multiple ways to make use of one product. Read and research, gather an audience and then present it to them. Don't focus on selling alone.

What is the role of social media in growing such a business?

I have never used Facebook or Instagram ads to get customers. Whatever content you post on social media, make sure it is useful to the audience. On days when one post does well, I attract thousands of potential customers to my website in one day. Post good-quality content, keep experimenting and get the hang of it. Use the latest trends on any platform to attract a bigger audience. The audience will buy your story, not your product. Make sure you show your face and tell your story.

Do you prefer to be an online brand or have a brick-and-mortar store presence?

Online presence is great. Start off with social media and a website. Amazon is great as a third-party seller.

A customer will not know my brand on a shelf in a store with multiple brands, and it is easy to get lost in the midst of hundreds of other brands, which is why building a unique online presence helps.

What is your advice for young people who want to get into such a homegrown business?

Right now it is much easier to venture into a business. If you believe that you will be the first person to buy the product that you launch in the market, then go ahead and launch it. It also depends on financial security. I started teaching tuition classes to fund my business. The first two to three years are a struggle. Have a good stream of income on the side, which also gives you peace of mind and reduces stress. Simultaneously, learn to use social media effectively as it can get you clients like no one can. Exhibitions and farmers' markets are also great platforms.

Projects

In this section, we will go through some simple recipes for hair and skincare that can be used in your daily self-care rituals. These are quick to make, using easily available ingredients and they make for lovely gifts for family and friends.

1. Green Goddess Hair Oil 178
2. Hair Wash Powder 179
3. Herbal Bath Powder 182
4. 3-in-1 Face Scrub Powder 185
5. Citrus Burst Sugar Scrub 187
6. Cafe Mocha Scrub 189
7. Quick and Easy Lip Balms 190
8. Body Butter 191

1. Green Goddess Hair Oil

A hair massage is a beautiful exercise in self-care, nourishing the scalp and the hair. Let your hair soak in the goodness of the oil infused with herbs and spices and wash it off with home-made herbal hair powder. The days I do this, my hair smells like petrichor in a forest. I cannot trade this smell for any of the commercial hair oils or shampoos, no matter how fancy the brand.

Customize the ingredients based on conditions you want to address such as frizziness, hair fall, premature greying, dandruff, itchy scalp and damaged hair.

Makes around 600 ml.

Gather

10 sprigs curry leaves (darkening, shine)
20 lime leaves (anti-dandruff)
10 hibiscus leaves (anti-hair fall)
5–7 betel leaves (anti-damage, shine)
2 tsp methi seeds or use 1 cup methi leaves (cooling)
600 ml good quality coconut oil
1 tsp edible camphor (increases shelf life, aroma) (optional)
100 ml flaxseed oil (extra nourishment, reduces frizz) (optional)
10 ml rosemary essential oil (optional)

Make

Wash, dry and roughly chop all the leaves. In a large kadai, heat 1 to 2 tbsp of coconut oil and sauté the leaves until somewhat crisp. This dries out most of the moisture from the leaves.

Blend it to a coarse powder and mix with 600 ml of good quality coconut oil in the kadai.

Keep this on the lowest heat for thirty minutes so that the active components of the ingredients are infused into the oil and any remaining moisture is evaporated.

Pass this through a sieve into a bowl, pressing out every drop of oil by squeezing this mixture. The residue should be fairly dry. Stir the camphor into the hot oil so it dissolves. You can also mix some flaxseed oil (50–100 ml) into this prepared oil for extra nourishment, along with 10 ml of rosemary essential oil for its hair benefits and beautiful aroma.

Store the prepared oil in a glass jar or bottle.

Notes: It's okay to omit the leaves that you cannot source. Other ingredients that you can add to the oil are moringa (drumstick) leaves, henna leaves and sliced amla. Keep in a dark coloured glass bottle to increase shelf life. Empty extra virgin olive oil bottles that are dark green in colour can be reused for this purpose. Make sure to wash and sun-dry the bottle well before filling it with this oil.

2. Hair Wash Powder

This is an aromatic, cleansing powder with lather that comes from soap nuts. It does not foam as much as commercial shampoos. This powder is naturally fragrant from vetiver and shikakai. When used to wash oiled hair, the powder leaves it cleansed without making it too dry. If you have very oily hair, then increase the shikakai powder by 25 g. Most of the ingredients can be sourced online or from Ayurvedic stores. Tulsi, hibiscus and neem leaves can be obtained from the neighbourhood or friends' gardens.

Makes around 350 g.

Gather

2 cups tulsi leaves (reduces scalp itchiness, improves hair growth, reduces hair loss)
2 cups hibiscus leaves (conditioning)
2 cups neem leaves (antifungal, antibacterial, improves shelf life of product)
30 g fenugreek seeds (conditioning, gives slippage to the prepared hair wash)
50–75 g yellow moong dal (cleansing)
200 g shikakai powder (mild cleanser that washes scalp without stripping natural oils, prevents dandruff, split ends)
50 g reetha (soap nut) powder (lathering, easier to use the powder like a shampoo)
50 g amla powder (rich in vitamin C and antioxidants, darkens the hair, reduces premature greying)
25 g vetiver powder (aroma, antibacterial)

Make

Spread the yellow moong dal in a tray and sun-dry for one to two days. Wash and dry tulsi leaves, hibiscus leaves, neem leaves and fenugreek seeds in the sun for one to two days until there is absolutely no moisture in the ingredients, and they are dried to a crisp. Any residual moisture will reduce the shelf life of the powder.

Grind the dried ingredients to a fine powder. In a large bowl, combine along with shikakai, reetha, amla and vetiver powder. The hair wash powder is ready.

Storage and use

Store in an airtight bottle in a cool, dry and dark place.

Use 3 to 4 tbsp of the powder, depending on the length of your hair and how oily it is. Mix the powder with water in a bowl to make a thin mixture. Apply well on a wet scalp and hair. Leave it on for a few minutes and wash off well.

Notes:

If it is tough for you to source all the ingredients, then a decent hair wash powder can also be made using just shikakai, amla, reetha and hibiscus, all of which are easily available in powder form. To start with, you can make a smaller batch and see how it works for your kind of hair, customizing the quantity of ingredients used as per your need. You can also experiment with other herbs like rosemary, curry leaves, dried rose petals, dried butterfly blue pea flowers and so on. Hard to grind ingredients like vetiver root can be obtained in powder form.

Although there are no staining ingredients in this powder, it is best to wash off any small splatters of the paste as soon as you are done washing your hair. The ingredients will not clog the drain or pollute ground water.

3. Herbal Bath Powder

If you find making your own soaps to be somewhat intimidating, then start with this aromatic herbal bath powder. Most of the ingredients needed for this recipe are herbs, roots, dried flowers, bark, etc., which are traditionally found in Ayurvedic stores. You will find many of these ingredients online these days. Do note that if using whole ingredients, it is best to get them ground in a flour mill. A high-powered blender will grind them too, but the powder will need to be sieved a couple of times to remove larger particles, which can be abrasive to the skin.

The combination of these natural herbal aromas is incredibly uplifting and soothing. If you so like, a few drops of rosemary or rose essential oil can be mixed into the powder.

Makes around 800 g.

Gather

500 g masoor dal (split, skinned) (base powder, mild exfoliant)
50 g *aavarampoo* (Tanner's cassia flowers; hydrating, cooling, antioxidant-rich, gives a glow)
50 g black sesame seed (for smoother skin, natural oils, exfoliant)
50 g kasturi manjal, sliced (curcuma aromatica/wild turmeric; this variety of turmeric is lighter in colour,

non-staining and with a strong fragrance like that of camphor. Reduces pigmentation, lightens scars)

50 g *poolankizhangu*, sliced (white turmeric; removes scars, brightens skin)

20 g dried rose petals (fragrance and cooling, soothes irritated skin, moisturizes dry skin)

20 g neem powder or 2–3 handfuls of neem leaves (antibacterial, antifungal, increases shelf life of the powder)

50 g camphor (such as *bhimseni* camphor suitable for skin application; alleviates pain and swelling, relieves redness and rashes, has a relaxing aroma, increases the shelf life of the powder)

50 g vetiver root powder (the aroma is calming, reduces stress, anxiety and insomnia; relieves aches and pains, antimicrobial)

Make

The best way to make this powder is to sun-dry the dal, aavarampoo, sesame seeds, wild turmeric, white turmeric and rose petals for one to two days until completely free of moisture.

Grinding in flour mill

The sun dried are best ground to a fine powder in a flour mill as a home mixer may not be up to the job. Combine with the neem powder, finely powdered camphor and vetiver root powder.

Grinding at home

Slicing the wild turmeric and white turmeric before sun-drying makes it easier to grind at home, instead of trying to grind them whole. Grind all the sun-dried ingredients to a fine powder. Sieve and grind the coarse particles in a small spice grinder. Sieve again and discard any larger sized particles as they may be abrasive to the skin. In the final grinding stage, add the neem powder, camphor and vetiver root powder to the mixer and give it a final pulse.

Storage and use

This recipe makes a large quantity of bath powder and it is important to store it safely. Neem and camphor are both useful in preventing worms or weevils from infesting the powder. To be doubly careful, pack it in a resealable bag and freeze or store in the fridge. Keep only a small quantity in an airtight jar for everyday use and use a clean dry spoon.

Put 2 tablespoons of powder in a cup. Mix in enough water to get a thick paste. Mix in cream or milk for dry skin. Let this sit for five minutes or so. Apply on wet skin, scrubbing gently. Wash off like you would soap.

Notes:

All these ingredients are also available in powder form in Ayurvedic stores or online. You can source the hard-to-grind ingredients in powder form and then combine with the dal and any other sun-dried ingredients to make a powder.

4. 3-in-1 Face Scrub Powder

This aromatic face scrub is ready in a matter of minutes. It is ideal to make a small bottle at a time as it does not take too much effort to make. This multipurpose powder can be used as a face wash, scrub or mask. Adding finely crushed rose petals gives a lovely aroma to this powder.

Makes 1 cup.

Gather

¼ cup fine gram flour (removes tanning, gentle exfoliant, reduces oiliness)
¼ cup oatmeal powder (soothing, reduces redness and irritation)
2 tbsp kasturi manjal powder (curcuma aromatica/ wild turmeric)
2 tbsp dried rose petals (aroma, soothing)
3 tbsp orange peel powder (exfoliant, skin brightening, aroma)
1 tbsp neem powder (antifungal, antibacterial, preservative)

Make

Take all the ingredients in a small, clean mixer jar and pulse a few times to crush the rose petals and combine all the ingredients.

To use

Take 1 to 2 teaspoons of the powder in a bowl. Mix with 1 teaspoon rose water for oily skin to get a thick paste. Mix with raw milk or cream instead for dry skin.

For face wash, wash face with water. Rub the paste lightly all over your face and neck, wash off and pat dry.

For face scrub, wash face with water. Scrub the paste gently all over the face and neck, being extra gentle around the eyes. Wash off well and pat dry.

For the mask, take 2 teaspoons of the powder. Mix in rose water, raw milk or yoghurt and apply a thick layer over your face and neck. Leave it on for fifteen minutes. Wash off with gentle scrubbing. Apply rose water or a light moisturizer after drying the face and neck.

Add-ons

2–3 drops of rosehip oil while mixing. Rosehip oil helps erase scars and pigmentation.

Body Scrubs

When I went to the US for the first time, I was enamoured by the bath and beauty shops. These shops have a way of calling out to you as soon as you enter the malls. The delightful fragrances wafting from them drag you in with invisible hands, making you want to say, 'Here, take all my money.' The promise of a more beautiful, sweet-smelling and softer you is all too alluring. Add to that an indulgent husband who would buy a jar of sugar scrub for over $20 without batting an eyelid (and I'm talking fifteen years ago).

When I attended a soap-making workshop seven years ago, as a bonus, we also learnt how to make face and body scrubs. It was a lightbulb moment, a guilty moment, all rolled into one, that all the ingredients for superb, all-natural scrubs are available right here, on our kitchen shelves.

Salt and sugar scrubs are some of the best natural scrubs you can make. And what makes these scrubs gentle on your skin is good quality oil. I make my scrubs with organic virgin coconut oil and extra virgin olive oil.

Why organic, you may ask. After all, it is only for the skin! The very premise of making these scrubs at home is to avoid the chemicals and preservatives in the store-bought scrubs. Choosing organic as far as possible in these DIY beauty potions just makes them that much more amazing. Scrubbing your face with a pinch of this scrub and washing it off with warm water makes it silken soft, and you can bask in the glow of not having used a single chemical on your skin.

5. Citrus Burst Sugar Scrub

The sugar acts as a gentle exfoliant, the olive oil provides a moisturizing effect, and the orange essential oil makes it an aromatherapy experience.

Makes one cup.

Gather

½ cup organic sugar
½ cup organic extra virgin olive oil
4–6 drops orange essential oil
1-cup glass jar or 4 smaller jars

Make

In a clean mixer jar, pulse the sugar two to three times so the granules are broken down to a very small size.

In a bowl, mix the ground sugar, olive oil and essential oil with a wooden spoon.

Sterilize a 1-cup glass jar or four small ones by microwaving on high for one minute, or wipe the inside of the glass jar with some rubbing alcohol on a tissue.

Fill the scrub in the jar and cover with an airtight lid.

Use

Wash the face clean of any make-up. Take a fingertip-sized pinch of the scrub and gently scrub face in circles until the sugar dissolves. Wash with warm water and pat dry. Do not wash off with soap, unless you have excessively oily skin.

To use as a body scrub, take 1 to 2 tsp, rub on elbows, knees, heels and any other dry areas, shower with warm water to wash off.

For most skin types, this scrub can be used once or maximum twice a week, especially in winters, however tempting it may be to use it more often.

6. Cafe Mocha Scrub

The coconut sugar acts as an exfoliant. The cocoa has an antioxidant effect and coffee is known for its anti-cellulite effect. The vanilla extract gives this a delicious edible aroma. The olive oil provides an intense moisturization to the skin.

Makes around 1 cup.

Gather

½ cup organic coconut sugar (alternative: brown sugar)
½ cup organic virgin coconut oil
1 tbsp cocoa powder
1 tbsp finely ground coffee (not instant coffee)
4–6 drops vanilla extract or 1 tsp ground cinnamon
1-cup glass jar or 4 smaller jars

Make

If using brown sugar, in a clean mixer jar, pulse the sugar two to three times so the granules are broken down to a very small size.

In a bowl, mix all ingredients and stir well with a wooden spoon.

Sterilize a 1-cup glass jar or 4 small ones by microwaving on high for one minute, or wipe the inside of the glass jar with some rubbing alcohol on a tissue.

Fill the scrub in the jar and cover with an airtight lid.

Use

Please follow the same process as mentioned under 'Use' for the Citrus Burst Sugar Scrub on page 188.

7. Quick and Easy Lip Balms

This the fastest DIY project in this book and it makes for a lovely little gift to go as part of a hamper or for visiting guests. It does not use petroleum jelly or chemical colouring. We do end up ingesting the lip balm so best to use edible natural food colours and flavours to keep it safe for use on the lips.

Makes 2–3 small jars.

Gather

3 tbsp beeswax pellets
2 tbsp shea butter
3 tbsp coconut oil
1 tbsp castor oil
2 capsules vitamin E oil
1 tsp beetroot powder OR 4–5 drops natural red food colouring
4–5 drops peppermint food essence

1–2 disposable wooden ice cream sticks for stirring
2-3 small glass jars (reuse the single serving jam jars or small cosmetic containers, or these can be ordered online)

Make

In a microwave-safe bowl, take the beeswax and shea butter. Microwave in ten- to twenty-second bursts for forty to fifty seconds or until everything is melted.

Mix the coconut oil and castor oil into the melted mixture.

Snip the end of the vitamin E oil capsule and squeeze it into the mixture.

Add the beetroot powder and stir constantly so there are no lumps. Mix in the peppermint essence and stir well. The mixture will start thickening at room temperature so keep the jars ready. Fill the mixture into the jars and seal well. The lip balms will solidify on cooling.

For cocoa lip balm, add cocoa powder instead of beetroot powder and use chocolate, almond or vanilla essence instead.

8. Body Butter

The shelf life of these butters is eight to nine months in a cool dark place. You can extend it by adding a vitamin E oil capsule. The antioxidant property of vitamin E acts as a preservative. It lasts longer if refrigerated.

In colder countries, the body butter recipes prescribe equal parts of oil and butter, but a 70:30 ratio of butter to oil works better in our tropical weather. These make for excellent gifts that take hardly any time or effort to put together.

Makes a 200 g jar.

Gather

Rubbing alcohol and tissue
250 ml glass jar
140 g shea butter
60 g olive oil
1 capsule vitamin E oil
2 tsp cornstarch or arrowroot powder
2–3 drops of essential oil of your liking

Make

Sterilize the jar by microwaving on high for one minute or wipe the inside of the glass jar with some rubbing alcohol on a tissue.

In a double boiler, melt the shea butter in a large bowl over a low heat until it is a liquid. Stir in the olive oil. Snip and squeeze the vitamin E oil capsule into this. Add cornstarch and essential oil and stir well. The cornstarch gives good spreadability and cuts down excess greasiness when applied to the skin.

Using a hand blender, blend this until you get a uniformly blended mixture. Put this bowl with the mixture in the freezer for one hour. Beat the chilled mixture using a hand blender until you get the consistency of whipped cream.

With a clean, dry spoon, transfer the body butter into the bottle and close the lid tightly. Label the jar with the name of the product and the date of mixing. It can be used instantly.

Store in a cool dry place or in the fridge in hotter weather. If you leave it out in the sun or a hot place, the butter will melt and the body butter will get oily.

Chapter 6

Lather Up

*'Soap and water and common sense are the
best disinfectants.'*
—William Osler

A profusion of herbs and flowers are in my kitchen
garden would want me to preserve them in some way.
Home-made soaps seemed the perfect segue for these
botanicals.

In 2014, I saw a poster for a soap-making
workshop in Bengaluru. It was on a Sunday, spread
over six hours with a lot of hands-on techniques along
with other good stuff like bath salts, body scrubs,
etc. It seemed like an immersive learning session, and
I signed up for it.

I started using the knowledge acquired in the
workshop almost immediately after procuring all the

essential supplies to make batches of soaps using my favourite essential oils and botanicals from my garden.

I haven't used a store-bought soap on my skin for the past seven years. I may have bought soaps just to satisfy the urge to try out something new, but I keep going back to the box where I store my home-made soaps. Even the commercial ones that claim to have 25 per cent moisturizer leave my skin extremely dry. My home-made soaps have freed me of the dry skin problem for good. The joy of making and using handmade soaps is something I want you to experience—for their gentle nature that doesn't strip away the skin's moisture, for their natural fragrances and colours and for the one less thing we need to buy that's wrapped in plastic packaging.

History of Soaps

There is evidence of humans producing soap-like substances in Babylon in 2800 BCE. A formula for soap comprising water, alkali and cassia oil was found written on a clay tablet dating back to around 2200 BCE in Babylon.

In the early times, the alkali used for making soaps from lard or olive oil was usually potash, obtained from burning wood or vegetables. In Syria, soap made by combining olive oil with alkali and lime was exported to the other parts of the Arab world as well as to Europe. Aleppo soap, a hard soap bar associated with Aleppo, a city in Syria, is made using olive oil and laurel oil.

Some of the other well-known soaps are Marseille and Castile soap. Marseille soap is made from vegetable oils, produced in Marseille in France for 600 years, traditionally made from water from the Mediterranean

Sea, olive oil and alkaline ash. The origins of Castile soap go back to the times of the Aleppo soap in Syria. Crusaders brought Aleppo soap to Europe in the eleventh century, after which its production extended to the whole Mediterranean region. As the early soap-makers around the Mediterranean Sea did not have access to laurel oil, they made soap using just olive oil and it came to be called Castile soap.

Why Make Soap

1. Soap-making is not just for homesteaders. We in our urban households can experience the joy of making our soaps and using them too. You can formulate your soaps depending on your skin's needs, the volume of lather you like, your favourite colours, fragrances and add-ins.

2. The difference between a soap and a detergent is that soap is formed when oils and fats react with a base and detergent is made by combining chemical compounds. You can make soaps to suit all cleaning needs and reduce usage of detergents significantly. Making soaps for handwashing, bathing, dishwashing, clothes washing, etc., at home is a sustainable practice as these soaps are gentler on the environment.

3. Commercially sold soaps are cheaply available, and they are filled with chemicals that affect the skin. Some of these are DEA, isopropyl alcohol, BHT, triclosan, petroleum products and foaming agents. Many of these are chemicals that should not be used on our bodies. Chemicals in these soaps and detergents also pollute groundwater.

All these chemicals can be bypassed when you make soaps at home.

4. Glycerine is a natural by-product of soap-making. It is a humectant, which means it attracts moisture into the skin and prevents it from drying, itching and ageing. In home-made soaps, the glycerine produced in the process of soap making is fully retained within the soap. In commercial soaps, this glycerine is extracted and sold to the cosmetic industry. In some soaps, a small portion of glycerine is added back.

5. You get to use the best-quality oils, essential oils and other ingredients in home-made soaps. Custom-making soaps as per your skin type by using specific oil combinations, herbs, essential oils, colours, exfoliants, etc. is great fun. You can make these as luxurious as you want with the addition of goat's milk, shea butter, avocado oil, jojoba oil, etc., which are rarely used even in artisanal soaps because they increase the price significantly.

6. Handmade soaps are the best gifts you can give family and friends.

7. Beyond all these tangible reasons, soap-making is a beautiful, creative outlet to make something that you will use every single day.

8. What do you need to make soap at home?

9. This simple high-school chemistry formula sums up the soap-making reaction and the main ingredients needed to make soap.

Fatty acids + base > salt
(oils)   (lye) (soap)

1. Oils and Fats

It was a revelation to me when I started soap-making that soaps are comprised almost entirely of oils, which form the backbone of the soap-making process. It's ironic how soaps are used to wash off oils when they themselves are made of oil. Soap is the result when oils are saponified by lye. For a basic soap, all you need is oil, lye and water. Commercial soaps go for the cheapest oils to keep costs down, and the most used one is palm oil.

When making soaps at home, you can choose from a variety of oils, depending on what you want in your soap, for their cleansing, moisturizing, lathering and other properties. The oils used also determine if your bar of soap will be hard, soft or brittle. Oils that solidify at colder room temperatures like coconut, palm and butters yield a harder bar of soap and those that remain liquid at room temperature give a softer soap. The combination of oils used is important.

Coconut oil, due to its high lauric acid, and castor oil give a fluffy lather that makes for a fun bathing soap. Coconut oil and palm oil have the best cleansing properties, but they will also dry out the skin if extra fat is not added to the soap (superfatting). These are also the best oils to use in detergent or laundry soaps.

Luxurious vitamin E-rich oils such as avocado, jojoba and sweet almond can be added in small quantities to your soap formula for an extra nourishing bar of soap.

Many soap calculators online indicate the quality of your soap when you combine certain oils with respect to hardness, cleansing, conditioning, lathering, etc., as well as the optimum percentage of each oil.

A standard ratio for a regular soap is 34:33:33 per cent of olive oil, coconut oil and palm oil respectively. Palm oil is the most used oil in the soap industry. The usage of unsustainable palm oil has caused considerable deforestation and habitat loss for several endangered species.

If you're making small batches of soap for personal use, I don't think it is wrong to use palm oil. Soap-making at home offsets a lot of environmental damage by saving on plastic packaging, preventing harsh chemicals from going into groundwater and so on. For larger-scale soap-making, sustainable palm oil or other alternatives need to be used. I have also used rice bran, sunflower, olive, coconut and soybean oil successfully in soap formulas.

The other option is to entirely replace the portion of palm oil with coconut oil, but then increase the superfat percentage (explained below) to avoid making a bar of soap that is very drying due to a high percentage of coconut oil.

Another easy formula to remember is 30:30:30 each of olive oil, coconut oil and palm oil and 10 per cent of another oil with desirable properties such as castor or avocado or sweet almond or butters like cocoa butter and shea butter.

Soaps can also be made with just one oil. Coconut oil soaps are good dishwashing soaps due to their excellent cleansing properties. Castile soaps are traditionally made with 100 per cent olive oil.

Here's a look at some of the commonly used oils in soap-making and their properties:

Oil	Hard/ soft/ brittle	Properties	Optimum %
Coconut oil	Hard	Excellent cleansing, lots of lather, big bubbles	15–50%
Palm oil (sustainable)	Hard	Mild stable lather, bars last long	25–50%
Rice bran oil	Soft	Mild cleansing, medium lather	5–12%
Sunflower oil	Soft	Mild cleansing, medium lather	5–12%
Olive oil	Soft, but hardens on curing	Low on cleansing, low on lather, very few bubbles	25–80%

Castor oil	Soft	Makes the soap dissolve in water more easily, gives more lather	5–10%
Cocoa butter	Brittle/hard	Lotion-like lather, long-lasting bar	5–15%
Shea butter	Hard	Lotion-like lather, long-lasting bar	5–20%

Resource: lovinsoap.com

2. Lye – sodium hydroxide (NaOH) or caustic soda

When I started soap-making, I had to hunt high and low to get lye for home use. This chemical is usually found in formulations used to unclog drains and sinks, as it 'eats through' any debris or clogging material. For soap-making, we need pure sodium hydroxide.

Some people will tell you that you can use drain cleaner instead of lye. While drain cleaners do contain sodium hydroxide, they contain other chemicals too. For soap-making, you need NaOH that is at least 98 per cent pure. When buying online, check the label for this information. Potassium hydroxide is the base used to make liquid soaps.

At the start of my soap-making journey, when I was looking to procure lye, an online search led me to a few chemical manufacturing factories in the vicinity. I called each of them, asking if I could buy a kilo or two of NaOH. Finally, there was one gentleman who didn't find my request ridiculous. He asked me to come over to the factory premises. It's not common for a retail customer to walk into manufacturing premises, but there's a first time for everything. I drove down to the industrial estate, found the shed and told them about my phone call with the owner. I was told to take a seat while they packed the lye. I was thrilled to find the key component that is required for soap-making, that too, close to home. Presently, you can easily find lye on Amazon or any other online soap-making supplies stores. Ensure that it contains only the one chemical we need and is not a mixed formulation.

Always be careful to keep the lye in a heavy-grade plastic box and not a metal box. Label it clearly with 'danger' written in big bold letters and keep it out of reach of children and pets. Lye will corrode the metal and any other surface the box is kept on. Plastic is the only material that makes it behave.

3. Distilled water

Initially, I would use only distilled water for soap-making as it was what I learnt in the soap-making workshop. You can procure it from chemical factories or petrol pumps. Recently, I have started making soaps with the RO water that we use for cooking and drinking purposes, and it works just fine.

4. Fragrance

What's a soap without a lingering aroma? One can choose between fragrances and natural essential oils. I prefer the latter over artificial fragrances, but that is down to personal choice. When I do the costing for soaps to understand how much a bar of home-made soap costs, the cost of essential oils is always much more than the cost of all the other ingredients combined. For small batches, you can buy pure essential oils in small bottles of 10 to 20 ml. When you want to make soaps more often, buying 250 ml bottles of your preferred essential oils from a wholesaler works out best. My favourite essential oils to stock up on are basil, orange, eucalyptus, cedarwood, vetiver and camphor. You can tell that I prefer woodsy and herby aromas over all others. When starting off, pick just three or four essential oils. You can use them singly or in a combination of two. Combining more than two essential oils may not always give you a pleasant result.

5. Colour

We love to see some colour in our soap. All commercial soaps have artificial dyes and colours. Plant-based dyes like beetroot powder, spinach powder or turmeric can be used in soap-making but most of these change colour when they come in contact with lye. Turmeric turns red, beetroot turns a dark brown and spinach turns almost black. Vegetable purees, micas and clays are other natural colourants you can choose from.

6. Digital kitchen scales

All the ingredients in the soap-making process are measured by weight and not volume, for precision. It is critical that all the lye in the recipe is used up by the oils. Any unused lye will cause skin burn and irritation, which is why the soap formula and the measuring must be as accurate as possible.

7. Pots and pans or plastic buckets

All the material for soap-making should be stainless steel, plastic or glass. An inert material like silicone can be used for moulds. Wood and aluminium react with the lye and are therefore not suitable for the process. A plastic or glass jug with a pouring spout is useful to pour the ready soap batter into the moulds with minimal spillage.

8. Candy thermometer

While you can make cold process soap without a thermometer, it is useful in the starting stages to know at what temperature you are blending the soap. The ideal temperature of lye solution and oils should be around 60°C.

9. Immersion blender (stick blender)

Theoretically, soap can be made by using any agitation technique that helps emulsify the lye solution and oils into a soap batter. However, stirring using a whisk or a spoon takes ten to fifteen minutes or longer, which is not practical. Using an electric immersion blender usually takes less than a minute.

10. Silicone spatula

It is useful to have a couple of silicone spatulas for stirring the lye solution and the batter and to remove every bit of batter from the bowls.

11. Moulds

Any box lined with parchment paper can be used as a mould. The easiest to use are the silicone baking moulds, be it loaf tins or individual muffin/cupcake moulds. You also get oval or round silicone moulds specifically for soap.

12. pH testing strips

These strips help check the pH of the soap, which should be at the optimum range of between 8 and 9. pH testing is not mandatory as an accurately formulated and measured soap will be in this pH range after adequate curing. pH testing strips are a fun tool for soap-making geeks. To use the strip, put a few drops of water on the cured soap and work up a wet lather. Dip the end of the pH strip into the lather. It should give you a reading of 8 or 9 as indicated by the colour change on the strip.

13. Safety gear

When making soap at home, 'safety first' should be your mantra. Gloves, an apron, a full-sleeve T-shirt, eye-protection or face shield, an N95 mask to prevent inhaling fumes, a thick plastic sheet and layers of newspaper to cover the countertop are the safety equipment needed.

The All-Important Safety Instructions

In the popular crime drama series *Breaking Bad*, Walter White, the high-school chemistry teacher-turned-drug lord, tries to 'take care' of a dead body by dissolving it in lye. He asks his accomplice to buy a plastic drum for this purpose. The accomplice takes a shortcut and tries to dissolve the body in the bathtub. The lye corrodes the tub and the floor in no time, and the half-dissolved body parts come falling through the ceiling into the basement. I'm extremely sorry for bringing up something so gory in a feel-good book, but this is all you need to never forget the importance of safety precautions while dealing with lye. Lye, in powder form or flakes, dissolved in water or in raw soap batter, all of it is equally corrosive, and requires handling with utmost care.

While working with lye, make sure there are no small children or pets around. Use an open-air space like a balcony.

Never leave the soap-making process unattended. Keep vinegar nearby to use immediately on splashes of lye water or raw soap batter. Vinegar neutralizes the effect of lye splashes to some extent. Always remember to add lye to water (as my soap-making teacher taught us—you LIE IN WATER) and never ever the reverse. Adding water to lye will cause a volcanic exothermic reaction that can be extremely dangerous.

While lye is a dangerous chemical, all you need to do is work with focus and care.

The Basics of Making a Cold Process Soap

Let me take you through each step in the soap-making process in detail. Read this part a couple of times to understand the steps carefully before you start making soaps. You can also watch some videos online to reinforce the steps.

1. Prepare your recipe, write it down and keep it handy. Use online soap calculators to formulate your recipe. Or use one of the ready recipes as provided in the projects in this chapter.
2. Set up your soap-making workstation in a well-ventilated, airy place.
3. Gather the ingredients.
4. Keep all the equipment ready.
5. Follow the safety precautions such as lining the counters with plastic and newspapers, and keeping apron, gloves and eye-shield handy. Also keep a bottle of vinegar handy to instantly remedy any splashes of lye.
6. Weigh each of the oils in the recipe individually. Use a silicone spatula to remove all the previous oil from the container before weighing the next oil. Combine all the oils in a large stainless steel pot. For example, if you are mixing 1 kg of oils for a batch of soap, make sure the pot is of

2-litre capacity to provide adequate room for mixing. Slightly warm the oils on a low heat until any solid oils have melted, and the oil is around 50°C as can be verified using the candy thermometer.

7. Wear the safety gear. Weigh the lye and water. Add lye to water, stir well, keeping your face out of the way of any fumes rising from the lye mixture. This reaction will release a lot of heat increasing the temperature of the lye-water mixture. Keep this in a ventilated space. Allow the temperature to drop to around 10 degrees of the oil temperature. The right temperature to mix for cold process soaping is 40–50°C, as read on the candy thermometer, which is why this is called 'cold process' soap making. Don't use a body thermometer for this purpose.

8. At this point, gradually add the lye-water to the oils. Start blending in small pulses using a stick blender. Stir using the blender between the pulses to check for trace (explained in detail in the FAQs that follow). Trace can be recognized if you pour some of the soap batter using a spatula on the surface of the soap batter in the pot. If the mark of this poured soap remains on the surface for a few seconds before disappearing, trace has been achieved.

9. The lower the temperature of the ingredients, the slower the trace. Keep blending patiently with gaps of stirring every few seconds.

10. When light trace is reached, add the essential oils, powders and any other add-ins. You can

also remove some soap batter in a small cup and mix the powder into this using a plastic spoon and then mix it in the whole batter to avoid any lumps.

11. Use the blender to mix everything for a few seconds.

12. At this point, you can transfer the soap batter to a glass or plastic jug.

13. Pour the batter into moulds. Tap the mould on the counter gently to avoid any air pockets. Using a toothpick, spoon or any other implement you can texture the surface of the soap. There are many YouTube videos that show these processes in detail. A sprinkle of oats, crushed seeds, orange peel powder, etc., can be done on the surface.

14. You can also reserve a portion of the soap batter to mix in a different colour or add-in and pour the soap in layers. The two layers can be kept intact, or you can create swirls with a small stick to let the layers bleed into each other. These decorative processes are a lot of fun, and you can experiment a lot. You can also press the bubble side of bubble wrap on the surface of the soap batter as it thickens a bit to create the imprint on the surface. This looks nice on honey-based soaps.

15. The soap poured into the mould needs to be kept insulated to enter the gel phase during which time the lye-oil reaction continues to happen, and all the lye gets used up. Do this

by placing a few layers of newspaper over the mould or wrapping it in a thick towel.

16. After twenty-four hours (some varieties of soaps can take almost forty-eight hours, such as Castile soap) the soap should be dry and hard. You can cut it into shapes of choice. For professional-looking soaps, check out the soap-cutting equipment available online. You can also use special knives called crinkle cutters to give a serrated edge.

17. Stack the cut soaps on a tray or wire rack on their narrow side so maximum soap area is exposed to air for the purpose of curing. Let these sit in an airy space for four to six weeks for full curing.

18. Wrap each piece of soap in a baking paper or brown paper and store in a box in a cool dry place.

Melt-and-Pour Soaps for Instant Gratification

These are beginner- and kid-friendly soaps. You don't have to buy too many raw materials and there's no lye involved. The soap base is already prepared and sold as blocks. The premade base is cut into small pieces and melted. Add your favourite essential oils or fragrances, colours and other add-ins and it is ready to be poured into moulds.

Swirls, textures and layers can also be made with these soaps. These instant soaps are ready to use as soon as they harden, as they do not need to be cured for three to six weeks as in the case of cold-process soaps.

You'll find different kinds of soap bases such as white, clear, goat's milk, etc.

Silicone moulds work best for melt-and-pour soaps as they can be unmoulded easily as soon as the soap batter has cooled and hardened. You can also buy loofahs, place rounds of loofah in the moulds and pour the melted soap base on to each round to make loofah soaps.

Melt-and-pour soaps provide avenues for endless creativity. You save time on preparing the soap from scratch, and it also involves less cleaning up.

Glycerine-based transparent or clear soap bases make a lovely canvas for herbs and other botanicals. A sprinkle of a vegetable-based powder like beetroot, spinach or turmeric shows off beautifully through the clear soap.

Suggested add-ins and colours for melt-and-pour soaps

A bunch of kitchen ingredients can be used as add-ins in melt-and-pour soaps that either provide antioxidant or exfoliating benefits. Botanicals add a touch of nature to the soaps. Natural colours from food help make the soaps vibrant looking without the addition of any chemical colours.

Some Points to Remember for Melt-and-Pour Soaps

1. Your soaps are only as good as the bases. Check the ingredients carefully before buying the base. There should be no sulphates or parabens in the base ingredients. Neither should it have artificial colours, scents, alcohol or any other unnecessary harmful products.

Add-in Ingredients	Natural Colours
Dried herbs like sage, rosemary, tulsi, neem or mint Flowers Activated charcoal Dried petals Oatmeal Gram flour (besan) Calamine lotion to make soothing soaps Crushed mustard seeds Crushed or powdered orange or lime peel Multani mitti Kasturi manjal (wild turmeric) Rose petal powder Aloe vera pulp	Cocoa Turmeric Spinach powder Pomegranate powder Beetroot powder Carrot powder Activated charcoal Kaolin clay

2. Melt the base in a microwave-safe bowl in thirty-second bursts.

3. Choose a mix of add-ins and essential oils or scents as per your need and liking. Allow the melted base to cool slightly before mixing in the essential oil as it may get degraded at high temperatures. The quantity of fragrance or essential oils to be added is usually 2 teaspoons or 10 ml per half a kilo of soap.

4. Extra melted cocoa butter, shea butter or coconut oil can be added to the melted soap base for extra moisturizing properties, especially in winter.

5. Use moulds that can take higher temperatures so they aren't damaged when you pour in the hot mixture. Any of the moulds used for baking purposes will do fine. Silicone soap moulds with individual cavities or muffin/cupcake moulds/ice cube trays are great for making melt-and-pour soaps.

6. Pour the soap into the moulds. These can be popped out as soon as they are hard and put to use immediately.

7. If the bar of soap doesn't come out easily, pop the mould into the freezer for half an hour and it will come out easily.

8. Given that the melt-and-pour soap base is already cured, these moulds can be used for food prep after they have been used as soap moulds after thorough rinsing. Strong essential oil aromas may however linger on.

FAQs: All of Your Soap-Making Questions Answered

Why use lye when it is a dangerous chemical? Why add this to your home-made soaps?

Lye has been used in soap-making for over 5000 years. Lye or caustic soda by itself lives up to its name in being highly caustic and corrosive. When combined and emulsified with oils in the process of saponification, the chemical gets neutralized to make salt. In a well-formulated and cured soap, none of the lye remains in the finished product.

What is a soap calculator?

A soap calculator is an online form in which you input the quantity of oils, water percentage, superfat percentage and you select the oils you want to use in the soap with percentage of each. The soap calculator will give you the correct quantity of lye and water to be used in the recipe along with the oils to make the perfect bar of soap. This is for cold process and hot process soaps only.

Can I use any plastic container as a mould?

You can use any type of plastic or cardboard container (lined with parchment paper) for your soap-making. Sturdy packaging can be recycled as soap moulds. Do not reuse these plastic containers for food purposes once used in cold process soap-making.

If you have to measure a plastic container, for a rectangular box-type mould, calculate the length, breadth and depth (reduce the depth by one centimetre to keep some space on the top of the mould, as you won't be filling the soap right up to the brim) on the inside of the box in centimetres. In the metric system, the total volume in ml is the same capacity in grams of soap that the mould will hold.

To get the capacity of odd-shaped moulds like silicone cupcake moulds or muffin trays, weigh the quantity of water that fits into the mould slightly below the brim. If you are using ten such moulds, multiply the weight by ten and that will be the total weight of the batch of soap you want to make. The quantity of oils used for the batch of soap will be 60 to 70 per cent of the mould capacity. In the online soap calculators, you will need to know the oil batch you will be using as one of the inputs (for example, 500 g, 1000 g, etc.). I learnt this simple but useful tip to calculate the volume of any container from Elly's Everyday Soap Making YouTube channel. This is my go-to resource for soap making.

Can I replace the oils with other oils in soap recipes?

Replacing one oil with another will affect the characteristics of the soap when it comes to hardness, lather and cleansing properties as each oil has different properties.

Also, soap recipe formulas are very sensitive as different oils need different quantities of lye, and the soap formula has to be recalculated by passing the numbers through a soap calculator.

What is superfat percentage in soap-making calculations?

Superfatting is adding extra fat/oil to your soap to add some extra moisturizing qualities. It is also a way of erring on the side of caution to have slightly more oil than is required for the quantity of lye so the end result has no leftover lye. This portion of oil does not get saponified and is available as an extra conditioner for those with dry skin. It is also useful for winter soaps.

What is trace?

When you mix the oils and lye using a hand blender, the mixture emulsifies and the soap begins to form. The start of soap formation is identifiable as trace when you lift the stick blender from the pot of soap batter and let it drip on the surface of the batter in a circle. If a trace of that circle is visible on the surface of the batter for a few seconds, that is the visual cue to stop blending any further and mix in the add-ins and essential oils. It is the reason why you should not blend the mixture continuously but just for a few seconds at a time and then stir with the hand blender to watch if it has traced.

The main thing to note here is that you want your batter to be somewhat runny to be able to pour into containers or moulds for the soap to set. Blending in the pan beyond trace will make the soap solidify and set in the pan itself.

How much time it takes for a mixture to trace depends on the oils used, the temperature of the lye and oils (cooler the temperature, slower the trace), the essential oils used (some essential oils like cinnamon speed up trace considerably), room temperature, humidity as well as the speed of the blender. This is why the essential oils are added only after light trace has been achieved, so they do not play a role in the soap seizing up prematurely.

Why is the soap in the mould not setting to a hard consistency?

Some formulas like olive oil soaps need up to forty-eight hours for the soap to harden. If you see oil separating out and the soap poured in the mould does not look uniform in consistency, then it may be a case of using the wrong formula or the wrong measurements with the oils exceeding what can be used up by the lye. This excess oil prevents the soap from hardening. Sticking to the formula and weighing accurately reduces the chances of bad batches that fail to harden.

Can we add milk and liquids other than water to soap?

Coconut milk, cow's milk, goat's milk, oat milk, almond milk, soy milk, coffee, beer and wine are some of the liquids that can be added to soaps. If you add a small quantity of these liquids like 20 to 30 ml, it can be subtracted from the quantity of water and added at trace.

However, there are soaps that substitute all the water with another liquid. The thing to remember is that mixing any liquid with lye causes an exothermic reaction, i.e., it generates a lot of heat. This could scorch the natural sugars in milk and other such liquids, giving the mixture a burnt smell. The colour may also change from creamy white to yellowish. To avoid this, the quantity of the liquid used (as a water substitute) is weighed out as per the formula. This is frozen into ice cubes.

When you are ready to make the soap, measure out the lye. Place the frozen milk cubes in a bowl that is kept in an ice bath (a bigger bowl with iced water). Add the lye one spoon at a time, stirring well to keep mixing and then add the next spoonful. The frozen milk, ice bath and the gradual adding of lye ensure that the temperature of the mixture remains low and the milk does not burn. As this is mixed at a low temperature, stir for a while longer to be very sure that all the lye has indeed dissolved in the milk. Any undissolved lye can cause burns or irritation to the skin. However, this is a more advanced level of soap-making. It is best to start your experiments with water and try out these combinations as you get better at the process.

How can we add salt and sugar to soaps?

Salt makes a hard bar of soap and sugar makes it soft. Salt makes the soap harder during the curing process, allowing you to use the soap a little earlier. A small quantity of salt, such as 1 teaspoon per kilogram of oil used, will allow you to get cured bars of soap sooner than usual. Salt is added to water before adding the lye.

There are soaps that are called salt bars that are cleansing and exfoliating. In this process, salt is added to the soap batter at light trace in large quantities—for example: 100 per cent of the entire soap batter (if the soap batter weighs 1 kg, then 1 kg of salt added) or 100 per cent of the oils used or 50 to 70 per cent of the oils used. The salt added to the soap batter is stirred well and immediately poured into moulds as it will start to harden immediately. The bars are also removed from the moulds or cut as soon as they harden, because salt bars have a tendency to be extremely hard and difficult to cut with time.

Adding sugar to soap makes it sudsier, giving more lather. This is especially useful in formulas with oils that don't lather much, such as olive oil. Sugar can be dissolved in the water first and then the required quantity of lye can be added to this sugar water. The quantity of sugar used is ½ to 1 teaspoon per 500 g of oil. You can also make a simple syrup with sugar and water in a 2:1 ratio and add 1 to 2 teaspoons of this syrup to the soap batter at the trace stage.

What is curing and why do home-made soaps need to be cured before using?

A soap bar needs to be dried out well before it can be used or stored. This takes four to six weeks. Two important things happen during the curing phase.

The saponification process is completed, making the soap milder and gentler on the skin. Evaporation of excess water makes the soap lose a little weight and shrink in size. It also hardens the bar, making it last longer in the shower.

Low-water soap recipes need a shorter curing time. Olive oil soaps need a longer curing time.

Do home-made soaps have an expiry date?

Home-made soaps are usually good for six months to a year, before the oils go rancid. However, I have used soaps for three years after their date of curing, and I have found them to be good.

What is the use of a soap journal?

Whenever you try a new soap recipe or formula, write it down in a notebook with the date, and if possible, include a picture of the bars. This helps keep note of the recipe if you wish to repeat it. It also lets you keep track of the curing dates. You can also make notes once the soap is used regarding its properties such as hardness, cleansing, lather, fragrance, etc.

What is hot process soap-making?

In cold process soap-making, the mixing happens at room temperature and none of the ingredients are kept to cook, except for the heat applied to melt solidified oils and butters. Hot process soap-making requires around an hour of cooking the traced soap mixture on the stove. While many articles and videos will tell you that hot process soaps don't need to be cured, they are best used after curing, so that all the excess moisture evaporates and the bar is hardened and develops a crystalline structure. The rest of the processes such as the formula, ingredients, mixing, remain the same as those for cold process soap-making.

Soap-Making as a Business

Rustic, artisanal soaps with all natural ingredients are a rage in the present times. With more awareness of the benefits of handmade soaps, this is a growing business. People who start off as hobby soap makers soon find themselves making dozens of batches of soaps. There's only so much one can use or gift to relatives and friends. If you are passionate about this hobby, there is a big scope to convert into a business.

Here are a few tips specific to the business of soap-making.

- Once you decide to move from a hobby to a business, don't continuously make experimental batches of soap. Select a few variants that will work well for your target market and stick to those.
- Don't buy ingredients like oils, lye and essential oils in retail, or in small batches. Buy these from wholesalers so you get them at cheaper rates and can improve your profit margins.
- Don't keep gifting your soaps to family and friends. Treat it as a business and value your product. Provide samples to boutique stores that will agree to buy lots of soap from you or give you a lucrative display in the store. You can also request dermatologists in your locality or circle to give your soaps a try and offer you valuable feedback.
- Research into the skin benefits offered by the botanicals that you will be using in the soaps. Talk about these benefits in the marketing material of your soaps, both online and in print, as relevant.
- The packaging of a soap is as important as the soap itself, especially in the times of Instagram. Get a good designer to design an eye-catching and innovative packaging for your soap, keeping it as sustainable and low-waste as possible.

Interview with Soma Datta of Zest Chest

After completing her doctorate in physics, Dr Soma Datta began her career as a soft matter physics scientist at the Raman Research Institute. But she took a break from her career on the birth of her daughter, after which she picked up cosmetology as a hobby, which then grew into a career of teaching and manufacturing.

Almost a decade since, she is now one of the most popular trainers in cosmetology and has trained thousands of students from across the world. She is also the co-founder of www.zestchest.com, India's first online training class for cosmetology. Her goal is to help anybody interested in cosmetology achieve success primarily by learning the fundamentals correctly and then building on that using one's own creativity. Her company also provides formulation, development and factory set-up support for manufacturers and brands interested in launching cosmetic products.

Tell us a little bit about yourself

I'm a cosmetology trainer and consultant, and I founded Zest Chest, which provides training, consulting and manufacturing services. I am a mom to an eleven-year-old daughter. I am also an avid marathoner and triathlete. My other interests include crafting, calligraphy and I am on the constant lookout for new things to learn.

How did you first get into soap-making?

During my pregnancy, I was working, but I was on the lookout for safe and healthy practices for nutrition and skin and haircare products. As I continued to research these, I became very interested in skin and haircare products. I started making soaps. There were no trainers or supplies for soap-making in those days. But given that I was working at a research institute, I had access to the most important ingredient for soap-making, which is lye or sodium hydroxide. I started experimenting, made a lot of soaps and body butters. After my child was born, I intended to use these for her and my family.

Over a decade ago, given that there were no YouTube videos, etc., how did you learn to make soaps?

I read a lot of articles and research papers online, and I learnt by making things myself, experimenting, figuring out where I was failing and kept taking learnings from there.

Why do you think people should try their hand at soap-making? What are the benefits of making soaps at home?

Just as we all prefer eating home-cooked food regularly, making soap has a similar justification. You have control over the quality, ingredients, you can personalize it and it is as easy as cooking. It can be made in the kitchen, and you can see the benefits of making skincare products at home.

What do you think are the intangible benefits of making something with your hands?

When you create something, it is your baby. You get pleasure out of making something and when your family and friends (or customers) use it and tell you that the product is way better than what they buy in the market.

You are always occupied when you are creating something, it is a sort of emotional release.

Mindfulness and concentration in soap-making is mandatory so those are the added benefits.

In soap-making, there are many other products one can make such as shampoo bars, milk soaps, botanical soaps, etc. Do share a couple of your personal favourites.

I don't like to make the same things on repeat mode. I like using what is available in the kitchen such as turmeric, ground oatmeal, milk, milk powder, and basic herbal ingredients like amla and shikakai.

I'm not a fan of very exotic ingredients. If you are getting into the soap-making business then it makes sense to explore more exotic ingredients as your USP and a differentiator from other brands. If I'm making soaps for myself, I like to keep it simple, picking up ingredients from the kitchen.

How did you think of getting into teaching people how to make soaps?

I started off by teaching chocolate-making and terracotta jewellery. While I would tell people that I can also teach soap-making, I didn't see much of an interest. However, I did put up a couple of ads for these workshops, which got people inquisitive, but not many people signed up. People did not trust the fact that you can make soaps from scratch in your kitchen. Slowly, the word spread, and the interest became enormous, and soap-making took over all the other workshops and it became my primary course to offer.

Before I started teaching soap-making, I had made many batches of soap, learning from the mistakes of each batch and making notes, gathering enough information for people to refer to in the form of notes, including troubleshooting and safety instructions. I also learnt in the process of teaching.

Do you think there has been an increasing interest in soap-making in recent times?

There is a huge interest in soap-making in current times. Nowadays people read the ingredients on labels while earlier they would pick up anything without checking. People are realizing the harmful effects of many cosmetic products. Diseases like eczema that were not common a few decades ago are becoming very common now. All of this has led to people taking more interest in where they can buy better skincare products or making it themselves.

Soap is something we all use every day, so if someone has the capacity or knowledge to make soap, they should definitely do it. It's not much effort, takes fifteen to twenty minutes, and it's easier than baking a cake. One batch can last for three to four months. Once people realize this, they get interested.

Along with this, the content on YouTube and handmade soaps being sold on online portals are more reasons that get people interested.

People often get started with melt-and-pour soaps—
what is your opinion on them?

Melt-and-pour soaps are gentler than commercially available soaps, but definitely not as good as making soap with lye and oils as in cold process soap-making.

Get the base, melt it, add some kitchen ingredients and essential oils, and you can get bars of soap instantly. The way you can explore with ingredients, and the experience of making natural soaps from scratch in the cold process is much more rewarding. It is like making pizza dough, the sauce and toppings, as opposed to using readymade base and sauce. You can get started with melt-and-pour, but there is a different charm in making soap from scratch using natural ingredients. You cannot customize the base oils or the ingredients in melt-and-pour, except for additives, you can only control the colour, fragrance and shape.

What is the best project to start off with?

Don't aim to make very fancy soaps in the beginning. Make basic soap with a basic combination of oils, don't use multiple oils—choose two or three oils, lye and some basic kitchen ingredients like turmeric or oats.

Don't try to make pure milk-based soaps as that needs some experience.

Make a simple soap, let it cure, use it and make notes on how the soap feels on your skin.

Slowly, you can make a couple of butter soaps like cocoa butter or shea butter and see the difference between the normal soap and butter-based soaps.

Once you've made a few batches you can experiment with colours, design, exotic ingredients (blue spirulina, clays)—something basic that does not break your confidence.

How do you constantly stay updated in this field?

Given that this is my primary business, I constantly stay updated with new trends, new ingredients, sometimes incorporating ideas from clients. I also try to cross-pollinate ingredients from other cosmetology products into soaps.

Anything I come across as a new trend in the market being used for some other purpose, I see if they can be used in soaps.

What are the avenues to get into business in this space?

Awareness and demand for handmade soaps has grown exponentially in the last couple of years. People want to use these products, but the supply is small as there are no big manufacturers of pure handmade soaps to meet the large demand. Even if there are many people making soaps, the number is not enough to meet the demand, which is much bigger.

The best thing about soap-making is that you can start small from a corner of your kitchen with very little investment. You can test out the soaps on family and friends and take feedback. Slowly step up and invest money from sales, get more help, take up more space and make soaps on a larger scale or grow to as big as a manufacturing plant.

Online selling makes it easier. Many of my friends and students sell handmade soaps on Amazon.

This is a business I would encourage anyone to get into. The investment is small. You can start with minimal equipment such as one round-shaped mould, a few oils, lye and essential oils.

Start with one variant and keep launching new varieties to grow in the line of soap-making and explore more products with time, customizing as per your requirements. I feel very confident about this business.

Training and educating people and creating video tutorials are some of the other avenues in the space of soap-making. But product sales have much better returns than training.

Any tips for those who want to get into the business of soap-making?

The most important thing is don't jump from making your first batch of soap to making it into a business.

Experiment, enjoy the process, research, read a lot, get thorough knowledge, test the product on family and friends, then come up with your best product, which is what you should give the world.

Projects

Here are a few simple soap-making projects you can start off with. The first one is a melt-and-pour soap that is ready for use instantly. The rest follow the cold process method which is explained in full detail earlier in the chapter.

Please be careful when using lye to avoid any burns or accidents. Read all the safety precautions, all about oils, lye, measuring ingredients, tracing and curing given at the beginning of this chapter before starting with these recipes. These are very important concepts that you must understand before starting off with soap-making.

1. Sheer Botanical Soap   230
2. Castile Soap   231
3. The Herbalist   233
4. Shampoo Bar   235
5. Dishwashing Soap   236

1. Sheer Botanical Soap

This clear melt-and-pour soap with botanicals inside is a visual delight. Makes for excellent last-minute gifts.

Makes 6 bars of around 80 g each.

Gather

Rectangular soap mould (6 in 1)
Microwave safe glass bowl
Silicone spatula
500 g clear glycerine soap base
Microwave-safe bowl
Silicone spatula
3–4 drops yellow food colour
15 ml eucalyptus essential oil
2 tsp coconut oil
Dried marigold petals
Handful of chopped eucalyptus leaves or rosemary sprigs (optional)

Make

Chop the soap base into small pieces and keep in a microwave-safe bowl. Microwave in 30-second bursts and stir with the spatula. Repeat until the soap base is fully melted.

Allow this to cool for two to three minutes. Stir in the essential oil, coconut oil and marigold petals.

Place the herbs in each of the six cavities of the mould. Pour the melted soap base in each cavity.

Allow to dry and harden. Pop out and these are ready for use.

2. Castile Soap

Castile soaps are traditionally 100 per cent olive oil soaps from the Castile region of Spain. During the medieval period, Castile soap was the most expensive soap money could buy, when access to soaps and baths was considered a mark of luxury. 100 per cent olive oil soaps have a very mild but creamy lather. These soaps are very gentle, and they leave your skin feeling soft and nourished.

Makes a batch of 650 g or 6 good-sized bars.

Gather

Silicon muffin moulds (8–10 holes)
4 medium plastic containers (takeaway plastic containers are fine too)
Plastic jug to mix lye-water
Plastic or steel bowl to mix the soap batter
Stick blender
64 g NaOH (lye) [accommodates a 5 per cent superfat]
95 g water
500 g pomace olive oil
15 g orange essential oil

Make

Safety precautions: Cover surfaces with thick plastic sheets and newspapers, wear gloves, apron and eye-shield.

If using a non-silicon mould, then line it using parchment paper and keep on the ready.

Weigh out lye (in a plastic bowl), water, olive oil and orange essential oil in different containers.

Mix the lye into water in a plastic jug, stirring gently with a spatula until dissolved.

Put the olive oil in another plastic or steel bowl. As the olive oil is at room temperature and not heated, you can start the mixing process without measuring the temperature of the liquids or waiting for the lye water to further cool down.

Pour the lye water very gently into the olive oil to avoid any splashing. Mix gently with a spatula.

Next, start blending this mixture using a hand blender or stick blender. Pulse for a few seconds and stop and stir for a few seconds. The mixture will turn lighter in colour as emulsification starts. Check for visual cues of tracing (explained in detail in the FAQs). Blending continuously may lead to you missing the crucial visual cues and burning the motor of the blender.

A pure olive oil soap does take longer to trace as compared to some other oils. Once you see a light trace, add the essential oil (or any other essential oil). Stir with the spatula for one minute or so.

Keep a sturdy cardboard under the silicone mould (I prefer silicone muffin moulds for this soap as it is easy to remove) so that it is supported when you move it and does not fold over. Pour the mixture into the mould. Cover with another piece of board. Cover this entire set-up with an old towel or blanket to keep the batter warm. This is to encourage gelling. Let this sit undisturbed for forty-eight hours (olive oil soaps take longer to harden and set).

The soap should have hardened in these two days and should unmould easily. If for any reason it sticks to the mould, keep the mould in the freezer for an hour and it should come out easily.

Keep the soaps for curing for a minimum of six weeks. Castile soaps have a long curing phase.

Once the curing phase is done, you can use the soap, gift it or pack it and store it.

3. The Herbalist

A hard bar of soap with flecks of greens and the herby aroma of basil.

Makes 6 good-sized bars.

Gather

6–8 bar silicone mould
Plastic containers to weigh all the ingredients
Plastic jug to mix lye and water
Plastic or steel bowl to mix the soap batter
Stick blender
72 g NaOH (lye) [accommodates a 5 per cent superfat]
107 g water
175 g olive oil (35 per cent)
150 g coconut oil (30 per cent)

150 g palm oil (30 per cent)
25 g castor oil (5 per cent)
1 tbsp spinach powder
1 tsp crushed dried basil
1 tsp kaolin clay
15 g basil essential oil

Make

Safety precautions: Cover surfaces with thick plastic sheets and newspapers, wear gloves, apron and eye-shield.

If using a non-silicon mould, then line it using parchment paper and keep on the ready.

Prepare the lye solution first so that it has time to cool slightly as you organize the other ingredients. Mix the lye into water in a plastic jug, stirring gently with a spatula until dissolved.

Weigh out the oils and combine them in a bowl. Make sure the coconut oil is in liquid form. If not, microwave it for thirty seconds or more until fully melted. Add spinach powder, dried basil and clay to the bowl of oils. Use a stick blender to blend these dry powders into the oils until the powders are well blended and no clumps remain.

Once the lye solution has somewhat cooled, add it slowly to the oil mixture. Mix gently with a spatula.

Now, start blending this mixture using a hand blender or stick blender. Pulse for a few seconds and stop and stir for a few seconds. The mixture will turn lighter in colour as emulsification starts. You should also be on the watch out for trace. Blending continuously may lead to you missing the crucial visual cues and burning the motor of the blender.

Once you see a light trace, add the basil essential oil (or any other essential oil). Stir with the spatula for one minute or so.

Keep a sturdy cardboard under the silicone mould (I prefer silicone muffin moulds for this soap as it is easy to remove) so that it is supported when you move it and does not fold over.

Pour the mixture into the mould. Cover with another piece of board. Cover this entire set-up with an old towel or blanket to keep the batter warm. This is to encourage gelling. Let this sit undisturbed for twenty-four hours.

The soap should have hardened in twenty-four hours and should unmould easily. If for any reason it sticks to the mould, keep the mould in the freezer for an hour and it should come out easily.

Keep the soaps for curing for a minimum of three to four weeks.

Once the curing phase is done, you can use the soap, gift it or pack it and store it.

4. Shampoo Bar

Save the earth from plastic shampoo bottles and chemicals going into groundwater and your hair and skin from harsh, harmful chemicals like parabens, SLS, etc.

Once you get used to shampoo bars, you will never go back to a commercially made shampoo. The two main considerations for a shampoo bar are good cleansing and good lather, which a combination of coconut and castor oil provide very well. A 5 per cent superfat keeps your hair from drying out too much.

Makes around 700 g or 7 bars of 100 g.

Gather

6–8 bar silicone mould
Plastic containers to weigh all the ingredients
Plastic jug to mix lye and water
Plastic or steel bowl to mix the soap batter
Stick blender
75 g NaOH (lye)
113 g water
250 g coconut oil (50 per cent)
200 g pomace olive oil (40 per cent)
50 g castor oil (10 per cent)
15 g essential oil (if using)

Make

Follow the same procedure as described in the earlier recipe (the Herbalist).

5. Dishwashing Soap

Coconut oil, with its excellent cleansing properties, makes for the best dishwashing or general purpose cleaning soap.

Makes a 1458 g batch, roughly 15 bars of soap.

Gather

Slim rectangular or plastic tray shaped mould
Plastic containers to weigh all the ingredients
Plastic jug to mix lye and water
Plastic or steel bowl to mix the soap batter
Stick blender
183 g NaOH (lye)
275 g water
1000 g coconut oil

Make

Make the lye solution as described in the other recipes.

If the coconut oil is not in liquid form, melt it by keeping in the microwave for thirty to sixty seconds. Stir to ensure there are no solid lumps.

Keep a mould lined and ready.

Follow the same process as described earlier to mix the lye solution into the coconut oil. Blend until you get a light trace and pour into moulds.

This recipe needs no superfatting, fragrance or add-ins.

Let it sit for twenty-four hours before cutting it into shapes that are suitable for your cleaning purposes.

Cure for three to four weeks before you start using these bars for kitchen cleaning purposes.

Chapter 7

Grow

'In the spring at the end of the day, you should smell like dirt.'
—Margaret Atwood

I was born and brought up in Mumbai. I spent nearly thirty-five years of my life there. If I had one grouse about this wonderful city, it is the lack of greenery except in very small pockets.

While the older homes came with generous balconies, with the skyrocketing price of real estate in the city, balconies or verandas became a luxury. This space started to get included in the rooms to increase the square footage of spaces that 'mattered'. The box grill around the windows was a quintessential Mumbai way to get an extra few square feet of space where unused or lesser used things could be stored away out of sight. It would sometimes end up being an eyesore for those in houses facing these windows. Some people would make the most of this box grill space and grow beautiful flowering plants. If nothing else, this space would at least be home for tulsi or holy basil, a revered house plant for Hindus.

I grew up in a home with big, beautiful verandas facing the Arabian Sea, then a flat with a smaller balcony facing a street in central Bombay, followed by a no-balcony existence and then back to a home with a balcony facing an abandoned plot of land. The west-facing balcony in my last home in Mumbai before we moved to Bengaluru gave me an opportunity to grow some of my favourite herbs around the year. It was my first exposure to gardening.

Moving to Bengaluru ten years ago gave me the gift of a terrace kitchen garden. I count it as one of my greatest blessings. The first year, we had a glut of brinjals, a few varieties of tomatoes, spinach and my favourite salad greens. It was a year of learning constantly about soil, seeds, organic fertilizers, organic pest control measures, what can be grown in each season and so on. It has been ten years of being an avid kitchen gardener, and I still have a lot to learn.

I like to have my morning tea in the garden. The company of my plants, bird song, the cool breeze and the gift of watching the sunrise sets the tone of my days. Plants, herbs and flowers are nature's selfless gifts to us be it for visual beauty or food or medicine. They are ready to grow and give at the slightest encouragement and support. Being in their company is one of life's enriching experiences.

Not everyone has the luxury of garden space, especially in bustling cities. But fret not. With a little effort, a balcony or windowsill garden can provide as much joy and fulfilment.

Plants with Benefits

People may think of gardening as extra housework, but it comes with a whole basket of benefits.

Mind and body

During World War I, horticulture therapy was one of the treatment modalities used on injured soldiers returning from war. Gardening exerts a positive impact on the mind. The therapeutic power of gardening comes from being surrounded by soil, plants, seeds and flowers, and being aware of the seasons, the path of the sun and the winds. It is an exercise that needs immense patience, acceptance, an understanding of the vagaries of the seasons and the ability to take failures in your stride.

Growing a few plants that are in season, watering them, taking care of them and then enjoying the harvest is a fulfilling experience. Once you get the hang of coaxing seeds to sprout and growing them into plants, that feeling of playing creator is an addictive high.

Mycobacteria in the soil increase the production of the happy hormone, serotonin, in the brain, which boosts mood and improves brain function. The mindfulness in this activity and the meditative aspect of it is another gain. Believing in nature's magic as seeds unfold into plants that go back to seed is a reaffirmation of faith and an understanding of the cycle of life.

Gardening that involves potting, pulling out weeds, watering the plants, raking leaves, etc., is a good physical exercise that anyone can do as per their age, fitness and capacity. Gardening in the outdoors also gives us our daily supply of vitamin D.

Tangible rewards

We experience nature's beneficence at close quarters when we grow our food. In times when most of the produce is either bought from supermarkets or ordered online, growing things like chillies, mint and spinach on a windowsill gives you access to a few things for your daily cooking.

While it is difficult to grow all the produce required for an individual/family, growing a little bit of the food we eat is a wonderful thing.

Money-saving

Herbs, salad greens and exotic vegetables cost quite a bit. Greens get spoilt quickly, leading to food waste as well as a waste of money. When you grow these plants, you pick only as much as you need when these leaves and herbs are at their freshest best.

Family bonding

It is also a great lesson and example for kids at home to see exactly how food grows, making them realize the importance of the food on their plates.

Visual beauty

Plants are the cheapest way to beautify your home, be it a herb garden on the windowsill or indoor plants.

Your Gardening Arsenal

Soil

People new to gardening tend to invest a lot of money on pots and seeds but don't give much importance to the soil, asking the local gardener to get a bag of any soil he can lay his hands on. When it comes to gardening, the one thing that is of most importance is soil.

Soil performs many functions. It provides a medium for germination, anchorage for roots, functions as a storehouse of nutrients and water, filters and stores rainwater, prevents flooding, acts as a buffering medium against pollutants and is a habitat for billions of living organisms.

Healthy soil results in healthy plants. The vegetables or herbs that you grow get their nourishment from the soil and we get our nourishment from these vegetables. Good soil is that important for our good health. A living, vibrant medium, a gram of soil contains up to 10 billion bacteria.

The texture of the soil used to grow vegetables should be well-draining and loose and not heavy and compacted. The soil used for your herb or vegetable garden needs to be full of organic matter such as compost that contains all the nutrients for healthy growth and nutrient-rich produce. Organic matter also softens the soil, allowing the roots to spread easily resulting in sturdier plants, as also well-nourished. Soil can be enriched with the addition of compost or well-rotted manure.

Soil should also have an ideal ratio of NPK, i.e., nitrogen, phosphorus and potassium, for good foliage and fruiting.

Compost or black gold

The joy of turning kitchen waste into a magical ingredient that promotes the growth of your plants is something to be experienced. A family of four generates quite a bit of kitchen waste from stems, leaves, peels, parts of vegetables and fruits that have rotted, leftover food, eggshells, mouldy bread and so on. Even with refrigeration and modern food preservation techniques, food waste is a real problem.

In most parts of India, garbage segregation is not practised, and the dry, wet and recyclable plastic waste are all dumped together into the landfills. 60 per cent of the waste generated at home is kitchen waste. Composting is a way to prevent this food waste from going into landfills. The waste generated from food goes back to nourish the soil and grow food, thereby completing the life cycle.

Seeds

There are mainly two kinds of seeds—open-pollinated and hybrid. In the former, the plants or crops produce seeds that will give the same variety of plants when sowed in the next cycle. Some of them are self-pollinating. The produce grown from open-pollinated seeds has more flavour as compared to that grown from hybrid seeds. Growing edible plants from hybrid seeds has the advantage of disease resistance and better yields. These seeds are more expensive as compared to the open-pollinated variety. Choose what works best for you. In general, it is more cost-effective to grow plants from seeds than buying saplings.

Pest and disease management

Depending on the plants you are growing in your kitchen garden, it is good to be aware of the pests and diseases that commonly afflict these plants. Organic gardening does not make use of any chemical pesticides. The methods used are agronomic, mechanical and bio-pesticides. Some of these methods include companion planting, crop rotation, sticky pads, light traps, water jet sprays, neem oil sprays, chilli-garlic tea, tobacco tea and fermented buttermilk.

The Different Spaces to Pursue Gardening

- Windowsill
- Balcony
- Front yard or backyard
- Terrace garden with raised beds or container gardening
- Common spaces in residential complexes
- Municipal parks, schools, abandoned plots in the neighbourhood
- Growing fruit trees as avenue trees in conjunction with the local municipality

---

Diving Deeper into Kitchen Gardening

If you are getting serious about kitchen gardening, it is worthwhile reading books written by experts. International books help understand the basic concepts while the Indian books set things in a local context, making it easier to adapt to our situations.

Below are a few suggestions to get you started.

1. *Organic Home Gardening Made Easy* by Sujit Chakrabarty (Notion Press, 2018)
2. *Grow All You Can Eat in 3 Square Feet: Inventive Ideas for Growing Food in a Small Space* (Dorling Kindersley, 2015)
3. *Rodale's Basic Organic Gardening: A Beginner's Guide to Starting a Healthy Garden* by Deborah L. Martin (Rodale Books, 2015)
4. *Organic Urban Farming, The Indian Way–A Comprehensive Guide to Organic Gardening for Urban Spaces in India* by Prabal Mallick (Self-published, 2018)

There are also various courses on gardening that you could take, although it is best to choose one with a lot of practical experience thrown in.

YouTube channels

YouTube is a treasure trove of knowledge in any genre and gardening is no exception. The following channels serve their audience with knowledge and inspiration. I attribute a lot of my gardening gyan to the creators of these channels.

- Gardening is my passion / Dr Surja Prakash Agarwal
- Daisy Creek Farms with Jag Singh
- Grow Joyfully, especially for its detailed videos on composting
- Suburban Homestead / Siloé Oliveira

How to Turn a Gardening Passion into a Business

There are quite a few avenues for passionate gardens to convert their hobby into a part-time or full-time business.

1. For anyone who is passionate about kitchen gardening, one of the avenues is to sell open-pollinated seeds. By doing so, you are also contributing to food security in the long run.
2. Setting up and managing gardens in restaurants, hotels institutes or corporate spaces—quite a few five-star hotels have their own kitchen garden these days for a regular supply of some of the more exotic produce
3. For someone who is able to put up a bigger investment, setting up a garden centre or nursery specializing in kitchen garden related plants and equipment is a great idea.
4. Set up a microgreens business starting off with your own apartment and community—it is a viable business as the cycle is very short, there

is enough audience, and you can start it in your residential complex itself.

5. In the sustainability space, people have started making bio enzymes for self-use as well as sale. A lot of the fruit waste from supermarkets or vendors can be recycled into profitable bio enzymes.

6. Teach the concepts of kitchen gardening via a blog, YouTube channel, online or in-person workshops.

7. Conduct workshops in schools, teaching kids the importance of growing your own food.

8. This is not a kitchen garden-related avenue but growing and selling specialized plants and arrangements like bonsai, succulents and kokedama that are hugely popular nowadays.

Interview with kitchen gardening expert Meenakshi Arun

Meenakshi Arun is a Bengaluru-based, full-time data analytics professional who has been an avid gardener for two decades. She is also passionate about solid waste management. She grows almost 80 to 90 per cent of all the fruits and vegetables eaten by her family.

Tell us about yourself, Meenakshi.

I am from a family that loved gardening. My mother and grandmothers always brought greenery into the house. Throughout my childhood, I had an interest in nature and gardening. I grew up in Dubai and Hyderabad, and I moved to Bengaluru after I got married. The environment in Bengaluru has always been encouraging for gardeners, sustainability and environmental awareness.

My husband and I are also passionate about Carnatic music. We are very involved in supporting artists and hosting concerts at home.

How did you get into gardening?

During my childhood, gardening was about growing flowers or a few herbs like curry leaves. I didn't know much about vegetable gardening. Like everyone else, I started with a money plant in my first home.

One of my earliest neighbours in Bengaluru had a corridor full of plants. Each time I walked past the corridor, I was inspired to add one more plant to my house. She was always happy to share cuttings. Another friend who was also passionate about gardening would accompany me to Lalbagh and many other nurseries. Once our balcony was filled up with plants, we extended our gardening to the terrace of the apartment.

There was a small farm near our apartment where we would go a couple of times a week to buy fresh vegetables. One of the evenings we reached early, and we saw from where and how they were harvesting the greens. They were growing close to a sewage drain. We were taken aback and that was an eye-opener for us. My friend told me that her mum grew all kinds of vegetables in Kerala and that we should try it ourselves. It was inspiring for me to start growing food myself. We started off with some greens like mint and coriander from the seeds in our masala box, and slowly progressing from there. I don't think I was serious about growing vegetables on a larger scale until 2010. That was when I came across Dr Vishwanath of the Organic Terrace Garden movement. I also came across the *Geekgardener* blog which had a lot of details on growing vegetables scientifically and methodically, all the way from seed starting to harvest. That's what set the ball rolling for me.

Do you think there has been an increased interest in gardening in recent times after the pandemic?

During the lockdown, people discovered that they had more time for pursuits like gardening.

There were supply chain issues during the lockdown and the plants along with other gardening materials started going out of stock in most nurseries. As markets and shops have opened up, I notice a lot of people in nurseries and garden centres. Instagram has also helped promote plant love.

This is a healthy trend as long as people are able to connect with nature and not get carried away by the whole exoticness of this hobby. You don't need to own every plant in the Amazon forest and turn this connection with nature into a materialistic pursuit.

If you had to choose between kitchen garden or foliage or flowering plants, which one would you choose?

They are all part of the ecosystem. My kitchen garden is full of flowering plants without which I would not get the pollinators like bees and butterflies—these are inseparable. There is also a lot of native foliage that is part of a shade garden system or where you want to add some colour. Among flowers, I grow a mix of native perennials used in my pooja rituals and annuals like marigolds or zinnias that are the pollinators. Each have their purpose in the garden.

As someone with a full-time career, how do you find the time for gardening?

When it's a passion, you just find the time for it. The kitchen garden needs a lot of planning, perennials don't. Summer is the only time we need to take time off the schedule for regular supervision. Most days I don't take more than ten minutes. On leaner days at work, I spend more time in garden maintenance. Monday mornings are my intensive garden days. Unless it is a large-sized garden, it can be easily managed without external help. A balcony garden needs just ten to fifteen minutes of your time daily.

What are the benefits of gardening?

Gardening is a full-body workout. There is quite some physical effort in a kitchen garden, such as digging, setting up beds, weeding and tying a trellis.

Touching and digging the earth connects you with nature and triggers a wave of feel-good emotions. There is a lot of joy when you see the results of that effort. A new life always gives you a sense of joy and hope, and it is true with plants as well.

What can someone start off with within kitchen gardening?

It is best to start with something we use in cooking every day. Fenugreek and mint are the ones you can start with immediately. You don't even need to get seeds for these. When you buy mint, use the stalks to put into the soil and within three weeks you will have the next batch. It doesn't need high-quality soil. Fenugreek can be grown from the methi seeds in your kitchen. Scatter these in soil and in two weeks you will have a crop.

The next step is to grow all the greens that you can use in your everyday cooking as these come drenched with pesticides when bought from a shop. Greens will grow in any lighting conditions, unlike brinjals or tomatoes that need considerable sunlight. The biggest change I noticed was when I stopped buying greens from outside, we stopped getting stomach infections or falling sick.

Could you share with us a basic checklist of things we need to start kitchen gardening?

- Pick your brightest balcony or spot by observing the sun patterns so you can place your plants in the best spot
- Get an optimal soil mix. Buy from your nearest nursery. I recommend one part each of soil, compost, manure and some neem powder for the antibacterial and antifungal effect.
- Always try to source open-pollinated seeds where you can collect seeds for subsequent crops.

- Understand how to sow, tend to and water your plants, and you are ready to harvest.

How do you constantly keep yourself updated?

These days it's very easy to find material on anything online. I follow a lot of YouTubers globally. I love some of the eastern European gardeners who operate under a lot of constraints, given the freezing winters. Videos from around India help me understand what thrives in different climates.

I would advise new gardeners to follow senior community experts in gardening who have an abundant knowledge in the field. They can join several gardening communities online. This is the best example of crowdsourced knowledge—especially Facebook groups where people can ask questions and do troubleshooting.

Projects

To get started with Operation Green Thumb, I will take you into six very simple yet fulfilling projects. We start with the most basic element of gardening, germinating some seeds, also known as sprouting and we gradually move to get our hands dirty to generate compost, which is also known as black gold.

1. Sprouts   254
2. Methi/Fenugreek Greens   256
3. Herb Container   258
4. Tomatoes   261
5. Banana Peel Enzyme   264
6. Compost   266

1. Sprouts

Sprouts are the easiest way to get the satisfaction of growing something right in your kitchen, using the ingredients you are sure to find in your pantry. It is the best thing to start off with. Sprouts can be easily grown even in kitchens that don't get much sunlight.

Sprouts can come from the seeds of a vegetable, grains or beans and are considered a miracle food. Whole green moong, masoor, moth beans and fenugreek seeds are all wonderful contenders for sprouting. Buy alfalfa seeds and you can grow these delicate sprouts in glass bottles.

Why sprout?

The process of sprouting wakes up dormant seeds by soaking them in water and coaxing new life out of them.

Grains, legumes, nuts and seeds have phytic acid, which is present as a plant defence mechanism. This prevents the proper absorption of nutrients when eaten by humans, which is why phytic acid is also known as an anti-nutrient. Soaking, sprouting and fermenting are the three ways to combat the negative effect of phytic acid. Sprouting leads to better absorption of nutrients from the beans or seeds.

Sprouts have abundant enzymes that are part of the metabolic processes in the body and help absorb the other nutrients in food better. Sprouted seeds and beans are rich in vitamins, minerals and antioxidants, making them a superfood that can be eaten daily. They contain up to 35 per cent proteins. Sprouts are excellent as part of a low-calorie diet as they provide a lot of nutrients for very few calories.

When grown at home, we can be sure of the hygiene and safety of sprouts by using filtered water to hydrate the seeds. When bought from less reliable sources, these may not be safe to eat raw in salads.

These are versatile ingredients that can be used in salads, wraps, sandwiches and omelettes. The thicker sprouts can be added to stir-fries and curries.

Gather

¼ cup green moong beans
1-litre glass jar
Strainer

Make

Day 1: Soak the beans in water in the glass jar for eight to ten hours.

Day 2: Drain the water by placing the strainer at the mouth of the jar. Add fresh water and shake the jar to rinse the beans well. Once again drain out all the water. Cover loosely with a lid and keep in a cool, dark place. Cover the jar with a dark-coloured napkin or cloth. This prevents the blackening of the sprouts. You can also keep the bottle in a large brown paper bag to cut off the sunlight.

Day 3: Add fresh water to the jar and stir well so that the beans do not clump together and rot. Drain all the excess water by placing a strainer at the mouth of the jar. Repeat this process another time on day 3, six to eight hours later.

Day 4: Long sprouts should be ready.

Once you have the sprouts, it is important to store them right to make them last a few days. Air-dry the sprouts for a couple of hours on a clean absorbent kitchen cloth and pat them try. Transfer to a box lined with kitchen paper and keep it in the refrigerator. Use within four to five days.

2. Methi/Fenugreek Greens

Methi leaves are one of the fragrant green leafy vegetables used in Indian cooking. Tender leaves can be used raw in salads. In north Karnataka, a delicious salad is made using raw methi leaves, grated carrot, coconut and onion tossed with a seed-podi for flavour and texture. It is best to grow these with seeds from a seed packet as they have a predictable germination rate. But to start off, you can use the methi seeds in your kitchen.

Methi will comfortably grow in a shallow pot of just 2 to 3 inches depth. Such planting trays, called bonsai trays, are available at nurseries and online. Any of the plastic fruit trays that have outlived their usefulness can be repurposed as a greens-growing tray. Make sure to poke a few holes at the bottom for drainage.

Rectangular plastic boxes that snacks or ice cream come packaged in can also be used, but given the smaller surface area, you will need to use multiple boxes to get a small harvest.

The potting mix for growing methi should be a combination of one part each of compost, cocopeat and garden soil.

Gather

2 tbsp methi seeds
1 shallow tray
Potting mix to fill the tray

Make

Soak the methi seeds in a cup of water overnight.

Loosely pack the potting mix in the tray, reserving a handful to top the seeds later. Water the soil well so it is uniformly moist.

Sprinkle the methi seeds all over the surface but avoid overcrowding. Cover the seeds with a thin layer of the remaining potting mix.

Using a sprinkler, gently water the soil. If you fear birds picking out the seeds, keep the tray loosely covered with a newspaper. This will also aid faster germination.

Make sure the soil is moist. Lightly water twice a day if need be, but don't overwater. In three to four days, the seeds will germinate. Water daily, but don't make the soil soggy.

In fifteen days, you will see a lush growth of leaves. In four weeks, the leaves will be ready to harvest. Using a clean pair of scissors, snip off the leaves with 2 to 3 inches of the stems. You can harvest three to four times using this cut-and-come-again method. Each batch will take another ten days for harvest. After every harvest, add some good-quality compost to the soil to help facilitate new growth.

Methi, being from the bean family, is a good nitrogen fixer in the soil. Once the harvest cycles are done, you can reuse this nitrogen-rich soil in other pots.

3. Herb Container

Whether you pronounce them as 'herbs' or 'erbs', these are the best things to start your foray into kitchen gardening. Herbs are usually required in small quantities when used as a garnish or for flavouring. They are often sold in bigger packs in supermarkets. The shelf life of herbs is quite short and most of them get wasted or lose flavour in the fridge. The best way to add a burst of flavour to a dish is to use herbs that are homegrown, snipped, washed and used immediately.

Choose the herbs to grow depending on the ease of growing and maintenance, and put together those that like similar growing conditions of light, water and soil. Most herbs demand two main conditions: good sun and well-drained soil. Soggy soil and shade is the easiest way to kill herbs. So beware of overwatering. Herbs are pretty maintenance-free except for the regular clipping that is required. Herbs can be grown in pots on a sunny windowsill or balcony.

There are hundreds of varieties of herbs and some like basil, mint and thyme have many varieties themselves. Choose the ones you love to use in cooking. Herbs have a number of uses in the home and kitchen. They can be used to make teas/tisanes, in-home remedies, bakes, vinegar, herb butter, herb-infused oils and in soothing baths and more. I love using the excess herbs from my garden in home-made soaps to give them a natural colour and texture.

The two categories of herbs based on their growing nature are perennials and annuals.

Perennial herbs will grow for a few years, and they do not need to be planted every year. These are hardier than annuals. Some examples of perennial herbs are mint, thyme, oregano, rosemary, chives and lemon balm. Herbs like mint have the territorial ambitions of Genghis Khan so they are best grown in separate pots and not in a mixed herb pot. Strongly aromatic herbs are also excellent companion plants as they prevent some pest infestation in other plants.

Annual herbs need to be planted every year, but most of them also self-seed. This means that the seeds that fall off from the mother plant will germinate if the weather conditions are right and in the presence of moisture. Basil, coriander and dill are some of the annual herbs. They are a bit fiddly in terms of growth requirements. For a new gardener, it is always good to start off with the perennials.

Most herbs taste best if harvested just before the flowering phase. When herbs flower, it is called 'bolting' and all the plant's energy goes into producing flowers and not the leaves. It is a good idea to harvest almost half the plant when the first signs of flowering appear.

Excess fresh herbs that cannot be used up can be preserved by drying. To dry small bunches of herbs, hang them from hooks or hangers near a windowsill or in an airy room. Herbs can be dried quickly in the microwave. Pluck the leaves alone and spread it over a kitchen tissue paper. Run the microwave at 60 per cent power for thirty seconds at a time until the moisture is dried out and the leaves are dried to a crisp. The dried leaves can be crushed and stored in air tight bottles.

To build a mixed herb growing container, choose a few easy-growing perennials like lemongrass, rosemary, thyme and oregano.

Gather

4–5 saplings or plants of the herbs you want to grow
A large terracotta pot, 12" height and diameter or larger
Well-draining potting mix

Make

In a large pot, place some pieces of stone to cover the drainage hole. Fill up to half with the potting mix. Figure out the position for each herb, somewhat like a class group photo. Keep the plants with trailing foliage like thyme at the front, taller plants like lemongrass at the back and medium-height upright plants like rosemary in the middle. This tiered arrangement not only looks aesthetic but also provides optimum sunlight to each herb.

Once the positions are set, place the herbs in the decided positions. You may need someone to help you hold each plant in place with the original soil surrounding its roots.

Put the potting mix all around the plants and press down firmly so the plants fit in snugly. Water the pot well so that the soil compacts a bit, and the plants settle down. Add some more soil if the level goes down after watering.

You can cover the surface with some decorative gravel or pebbles or leave it as it is. Every couple of weeks, provide an organic liquid fertilizer by mixing it in the water as per instructions on the bottle.

Keep picking the herbs regularly, which makes them grow more luxuriously.

4. Tomatoes

After herbs, tomatoes are the next thing you must get on to as a kitchen gardener. They grow well in pots. Six to eight hours of direct sunlight and well-drained soil are mandatory. If your windowsill or balcony fulfils this condition, then do get started with tomatoes.

In the markets or shops, we see two main varieties. In Bengaluru, where I live, one is the local variety, which is oval and less sour. Another variety called *naati* (desi), is rounder and much tarter. The varieties of produce grown to sell commercially are selectively cultivated for their shelf life and shape, not essentially for flavour. When you grow your own tomatoes, you can experiment with different varieties and make notes on what flavours work best in the dishes you cook. That is not the only reason to grow tomatoes. Plucking a vine-ripe tomato and adding it to a salad or rasam has an amazing flavour that a tomato stored for weeks in the fridge will not have.

Depending on their growth habit, tomato plants are classified as determinate or indeterminate. It is good to understand the differences and choose the kind of tomato you want to grow.

Determinate varieties have smaller plants less than four feet tall. They grow bushy with a lot of side shoots, Staking (supports with sticks) is not mandatory. All of the fruit is produced in four to five weeks and harvested in one lot. The growing tip gives our fruit and there is no further stem growth.

Indeterminate varieties are also called vining tomatoes. These grow to over 6 feet tall and staking is required for support. The plant continues to flower and fruit through the entire season. There are always fruits in different stages on the plant at any given time. The growing tip continuously gives out leaves and new stems.

Determinate varieties are good to be processed into pickles, chutneys and ketchup as the harvest is all at one go. Indeterminate varieties are more suitable for use in everyday cooking because it gives a regular small harvest around the growing season.

Tomato plants need regular watering. They are easy to grow, popular among kitchen gardeners and one plant can give up to 10 kg of fruit.

Gather

Tomato seeds
Small recycled plastic cups or seed starter tray
Cocopeat
9–12" pot
Potting mix
Compost for the growing cycle

Make

Fill four or five small recycled plastic cups like ice cream or yoghurt cups (with drainage holes) with cocopeat. Water this well. Make a small dent with a pencil or a chopstick and put two seeds in each cup. Cover with a pinch of cocopeat.

Water gently. Keep in shade and ensure the soil stays moist to enable germination. In three to four days, the seeds will germinate. In four weeks, the sapling is ready to be transferred to the pot. Stop watering the sapling one or two days before transfer.

Fill a pot with a drainage hole with the potting mix, which is one part each of cocopeat, compost and garden soil. Make an indentation in the soil. Invert the cup with the sapling and remove it along with the full root ball and the soil around it.

Place this in the well made in the pot and cover with more of the potting mix.

Water thoroughly. Keep in the shade for a day, then in semi-shade for a couple of days and then in full sun.

Tomato plants will take up to two months to start producing fruit.

5. Banana Peel Enzyme

Banana peels are an excellent source of potassium, which is one of the requirements for plants in their flowering and fruiting stage. Even if you don't have a kitchen garden, your indoor and balcony plants can also benefit from a feed of this nutrient-rich enzyme. If you are a family of four and bananas are a part of your daily diet, you will end up generating quite a quantity of peels as daily kitchen waste. These can, of course, be composted, but on their own make for an excellent tonic for plants.

There are a couple of easy ways banana peels can be used in the garden,

Chop the peels into small pieces. Sun-dry and powder them. Use ½ to 1 teaspoon of this powder per plant.

Banana peels can also be immersed in a jar of water, covered with a cloth and rubber band for two to three days. This strained 'tea' can be used in 1:1 dilution as a foliar spray or added to the soil.

Another method to use the peels is to make a banana peel enzyme, which takes three weeks but has a long shelf life of six months. Once fully fermented, it becomes a stable solution and a concentrated source of plant nutrients. Application of this enzyme promotes healthy flowering and fruiting in plants. It is one of the easiest yet most potent natural fertilizers you can make at home and feed your plants.

Gather

¼ kg banana peels
¼ kg jaggery, powdered or finely chopped
1 kg capacity jar (plastic or glass jar with a lid)

Make

Chop the banana peels into small pieces.

In a clean, dry jar, start with a layer of peels. Top it with a layer of jaggery.

Repeat the process to get alternating layers of banana peels and jaggery.

Leave 2 inches of space at the top of the jar.

Close the lid tightly and keep the jar in a cool, dark place for three weeks. Do not open the jar during this period as this fermentation process is fully anaerobic, i.e., occurs in the absence of oxygen. You can give the jar a shake occasionally.

At the end of three weeks, the peels would have disintegrated and formed a thick solution along with the jaggery, with a mild alcohol-like smell, indicating that the fermentation process is complete.

How to use

For soil application, use 50 ml in one litre of water.

To use as a spray, combine 1 to 2 tsp of the enzyme with 1 litre of water in a bottle. Strain this into a spray bottle using a tea strainer or cloth so that it does not clog the nozzle of the sprayer. Spray this on the leaves. Early mornings or late evenings are the best time for spraying this on the leaves.

(With inputs from organic kitchen gardening expert Meenakshi Arun / @meenakshi_arun on Instagram)

6. Compost

60 per cent of the waste generated in most Indian homes is kitchen waste. Composting is the best way to use the kitchen waste generated in your home to provide rich nourishment to your plants and keep the waste out of landfills. There are a lot of complex techniques, equipment and theories around composting. A whole book can be written on the same. A lot of us may be scared to get into composting given the perceived complexity of the process, the possibility of ants and other insects getting attracted to the compost bins and the rotting smell of food waste. What I'm sharing here is a simple beginner's guide to composting. Once you get comfortable with this, you can watch some expert videos and try out other techniques such as the Bokashi method, vermicomposting, etc.

Compost provides all three vital nutrients for plants, i.e., nitrogen, phosphorus and potassium. In a potting mix, it is good to have at least a third of the portion as compost. Container-grown plants will do well with a feed of compost every fifteen days. At the end of the fruiting or flowering season, adding compost to the soil will leave it enriched for the next season.

A good compost is all about the balance of 'greens' and 'browns'.

The greens or the nitrogen element: Examples of green waste are coriander stems, onion peels, leftover cooked food, coffee grounds, tea waste, fruit seeds and peels, overripe fruits, eggshells and vegetable peels. These are best chopped into smaller bits for faster composting.

It is not recommended to put meat-based dishes or leftover meat in the composting bin.

The browns or the carbon element: Examples of brown materials are dried leaves, grass clippings, cocopeat, sawdust, coconut husk, readymade composting bricks (cocopeat and microbes), which can be reconstituted with water and used as the brown element.

The other two important factors are culture and aeration.

Culture: Sour buttermilk or store-bought microbe powder/cultures to introduce a fresh batch of microbes to the pile that kickstart the composting process.

Aeration: Holes on the sides of the composting pots or drum are required for entry of air into the mix.

Gather

Large earthen pot with a lid
Kitchen waste (greens)
Dry leaves (or other browns)
Sour buttermilk (culture)
A long stick to stir the contents

Make

Ensure that there are a few holes at the bottom of the earthen pot. Place a saucer under the pot to catch any liquids that may seep out during the compost-making process.

Start with a layer of browns. Cover with a layer of kitchen waste (greens). Sprinkle around ½ cup of sour buttermilk over this. The bacteria in the buttermilk adds a bacterial culture that helps kickstart the breakdown of material to form compost.

Instead of buttermilk, a small quantity of cow dung manure or slurry can also be added to the mix. This is to help inoculate the pot with bacteria.

Do cut any large pieces like watermelon rind into smaller pieces. Crush eggshells before adding to compost. Transfer each day's kitchen waste to the compost bin. Keep this covered with a lid.

Using a rake or a stick, give the contents of the pot a stir to introduce air into the mixture around two to three times a week. Cover it with a layer of browns. Once the pot is full, keep it covered with the lid. You can also tie a net or mesh to the mouth of the pot to keep out insects. The liquid collected in the saucer below the pot can be diluted with water and used as compost tea feed for the plants.

The compost takes thirty to forty days to get ready. This depends on the weather conditions as well as the kind of waste added to the pot. The compost should smell earthy and pleasant, like petrichor. You will find a rich brown loose soil-like matter without any vegetable waste present in it.

This compost is ready to be added to the soil of your plants.

Notes: Keep the composting unit away from direct sunlight or rain.

Resources:

Swachagraha Kalika Kendra's Composting Learning Centre located in HSR Layout, Bengaluru, is a one-of-a-kind centre where people can learn all about composting.

Follow Vani Murthy @wormrani on Instagram for inspiration and know-how about composting.

Chapter 8

Fabric and Fibre Art

'There are many women who persuade themselves that the occupations particularly allotted to their sex are extremely frivolous; but it is one of the common errors of a depraved taste to confound simplicity with frivolity. The use of the needle is simple, but not frivolous.'
—Ladies' Needlework Penny Magazine

During the 2020 Tokyo Summer Olympics, among the many amazing feats telecast and reported, there was a heart-warming viral story featuring British diver and Olympic gold medallist Tom Daley. He made headlines for sitting in the stands and knitting while watching the women's diving finals. People's hearts were captured by the contrast of hardcore competitive sports and a gentle pursuit like knitting in an Olympic athlete like Daley. He has said that his 'love for knitting, crochet, and all things stitching' kept him sane through the competition. On his Instagram page, Daley posted a photo of himself with his gold medal with the caption 'Learning to knit and crochet has helped me so much through these Olympics and we won GOLD yesterday. I made a little medal case too! YAY!'

When I was a child, we had a hand-cranked Usha sewing machine at home, which was moodier than an adolescent kid. It would work as smooth as a new one at times, stitching entire curtains without a single hiccup, and then break down a dozen times for a tiny one-minute repair job. Just watching my aunts coax out stitching projects using this machine was a lesson in patience. The women at home used the machine for small repairs, alterations and new stitching projects. One of my aunts, having attended a stitching course, was adept at creating almost anything using the sewing machine, even bell-bottoms as per the fashion diktat of the 1960s and 1970s in Bombay. It was fascinating to watch a swath of cloth transforming into an outfit.

When I was just eight or nine years old, I was allowed to use the sewing machine. As it was not an electric one, it could only go as fast as one cranked the handle, so it was not dangerous for a child to operate. It amazes me as to how much freedom I got as a kid to operate machines. I would even go about fixing loose wires inside the plug of the iron, following the exact procedure as my grandfather did to get the iron working again. I cannot imagine letting my thirteen-year-old son open up electrical appliances and play with wires.

Back to the famous Usha sewing machine. For my sister's first birthday, I stitched a cute little frock for her with a small piece of fabric I found lying around at home, using a pattern from my imagination and some help from my aunt. I was eleven then. This process of design and creation fascinated me as a child. In school, the craft period was as important to me as other subjects. We were taught the basics of stitching. I remember being taught to hand-stitch a pair of bloomers (I mean, why?!) and a skirt (somewhat more useful, for sure). I don't think I ever hand-stitched a skirt for myself after the eighth grade at school, but the lessons I learnt did teach me that you can make almost anything with your hands. And that our hands are as capable as any machine.

A couple of years ago, I had the urge to buy a sewing machine and get back into stitching projects. The urge was spurred by the fact that it has always been tough to find tailors to stitch blouses for saris here in Bengaluru. Most of the tailors are the fancy designer kinds who charge more for the stitching than the cost of the sari itself. To test the waters, I borrowed an electric sewing machine from my sweet neighbour Uma, watched dozens of YouTube videos and managed to stitch my own blouse. A sari blouse is one of the toughest things to stitch because of the many measurements to take, the fit to achieve, the number of tucks and other components involved. It can be rather overwhelming. It was a huge sense of #achievementunlocked to be able to stitch my own blouse.

History of Sewing

Sewing started in the Palaeolithic era. Hunter-gatherers would stitch together pieces of hide or fur, leaving a hole in the garment so they could wear it as a poncho. It was one of the most primitive skills that the Palaeolithic people learnt, not for modesty but for survival in the cold. Small pieces of bone were sharpened to use as needles, and fibrous ropes were used as thread.

The indigenous populations of the American plains and Canadian prairies used advanced sewing techniques to construct tepees, a tent stitched out of animal hides, mounted on wooden poles. The more complex shapes of clothing came about after the invention of shearing scissors and metal needles, which was in the Bronze Age (2000–800 BCE).

Weaving cloth from natural fibres started in the Middle East around 4000 BCE, along with sewing of the woven cloth. Sewing was used for both mending and creating new clothes. Fabrics and stitching were expensive, so every item of clothing was used to its maximum. These were repaired, taken apart and reassembled, increased in length or girth and so on, in complete contrast to the rampant use-and-throw culture our present-day fast fashion affords and encourages.

From making rough ponchos out of leather and fur to complex embroidery work to embellish a piece of clothing is a whole spectrum of finesse in using a needle and thread.

Embroidery

Embroidery-like stitches were first used to repair fabrics using darning. These stitches, made in different colours, were then combined to make decorative motifs to adorn a fabric, which turned into a symbol of royalty, wealth and leisure.

While historically, embroidery has been viewed as a woman's pastime or leisure activity, it has also been used as a voice to tell stories in the absence of a formal education, literacy, writing skills or implements. It was a way for such women to document their stories through this art form, stories that would otherwise be unheard.

It is tough to trace the exact history of embroidery as fabrics do not survive time. Some of the oldest surviving pieces of embroidered fabric have been found in Egyptian tombs. The Victoria and Albert Museum in London has a collection of Indian textiles, which includes rare pieces belonging to royalty and archaeological fragments dating from the fourteenth century.

Embroidery of India

Embroidery in India has dozens of styles that come from different regions and cultures. The style depends on the texture and design of the fabric and the type of stitches used. Here are some of the well-known forms of embroidery from India.

Aari from Jammu and Kashmir and Gujarat

Aari is a painstakingly intricate form of embroidery, which is made using a hooked needle and a fabric mounted on a frame, the thread being fed from the underside. It comprises a version of the stitches used by cobblers to stitch leather shoes.

Banjara from Telangana and Madhya Pradesh

Also called *lambani*, this involves appliqué and mirror work making use of colourful threads to create vibrant designs. Fourteen types of stitches are used in Banjara embroidery, which is used to make the clothes of Banjaras, a semi-nomadic group who move around south, west and central India.

Chikankari from Uttar Pradesh

This was introduced by Noor Jahan, the wife of emperor Jahangir, using white thread on white muslin, fine cotton or voile, involving intricate floral patterns that use one or more of the thirty-five types of stitches. There are specialist embroiderers who work only on one kind of stitch.

Gota embroidery from Rajasthan

In gota, folded pieces of silver ribbons are stitched along the edges of a garment such as a sari, dupatta or lehnga, or are used to create designs.

Kantha from West Bengal

Also known as *dorukha*, this kind of embroidery looks perfect from both sides, and the fabric is usable on both sides. Traditionally, old and worn-out saris, dhotis and other pieces of clothing were upcycled into bedspreads and covers using the kantha stitch. Layers of recycled cloth were quilted together using this stitch, the coloured embroidery threads also being drawn from the edges of the old garments, a perfect example of sustainability. These days, the stitch is employed in the making of new saris, dupattas and other home decor items and not just for upcycling.

Kasuti from North Kanara in Karnataka

This is made using a single thread and counting the number of stitches. The two kinds of stitches used are *gavanti* (line or double running stitch) and *murgi* (zigzag lines using a darning stitch). Stitches on both sides of the fabric are neat and identical.

Phulkari from Punjab

Phulkari means flower-work. This form of embroidery has darning stitches made using colourful threads done from the reverse side of the fabric, leaving long stitches on the front side of the fabric. The dupattas are especially well known. Those with dense embroidery covering the entire dupatta are called *bagh* and are usually a part of wedding trousseaus, taking nearly a year to make.

Toda from the Nilgiris in Tamil Nadu

This embroidery done between red and black bands on the fabric is also called *pukhoor*. It has a finish so fine that it resembles woven cloth, and the finished fabric is reversible. It is a part of the Toda heritage and has a GI tag (geographical indication—a name or sign used on certain products which corresponds to a specific geographical location or origin).

Fibre Art

The term 'fibre art' is defined as fine art created using natural or synthetic fibre and other components such as fabric and yarn. The important aspects of fibre art are the materials, the manual labour of the artist and a product that is more aesthetic than utilitarian. Like other art forms, fibre art aims to convey a message and an emotion.

Quilting, weaving, knitting, crochet, embroidery, applique work, macramé, lace-making and tapestry are some examples of fibre art, the aim being to create beautiful art that tells a story.

Traditionally, fibres were used to make functional objects, but after World War II, fibre art started emerging. The term fibre art was coined in the 1950s as several artists in this field received recognition for their work. It was in this period that the 'craft artists' inspired weavers to explore working with fibres beyond just creating functional objects and to create works of art. The next two decades saw an international revolution in fibre art fuelled by the rise of the women's movement and the evolution of postmodernism theory.

Women and Fibre Arts

Sewing, knitting, crochet and embroidery are almost entirely seen as a woman's domain, although in the professional setting, there are many male tailors and fashion designers. It is the reason why a male Olympic athlete seen knitting shattered hundreds of years of gender stereotyping of these crafts.

Someone working on a laptop is seen as more skilled or qualified than someone working with their hands. The number of women spending their free time on crafts like crochet or embroidery has reduced significantly as women are now out there in workplaces and managing the home, leaving them with no time for such leisure activities. Anab Naiyar of Oony by Anab makes a valid point that women no longer have the luxury of free time once the household chores are done, to relax with some knitting or embroidery in solitude or in the company of other women. Women spending their free time productively has been seen as a virtue, which is why having fun at kitty parties is seen as a frivolous activity. The onus of productivity even in leisure is a burden women carry. This is worth thinking about.

Besides gender, these crafts were also associated with sweet old grannies who had a lot of free time on hand. Perceptions are changing rapidly with crochet and knitting increasingly being taken up by younger folk, those who are doing it for the numerous emotional and mental health benefits and making a business out of it too.

Anita Cazzola in her paper[8] 'Feminist Fibre Art: Tracing the History of Feminine Subversion' writes about how the world has never given women-made intricate handcrafted fibre art its due. When Lenore Tawney (1907–2007), an American artist known for her groundbreaking work in fibre art, exhibited her weaving at a self-titled art show in 1961, it was the first time that stitching found itself in the rarefied male-dominated realm of high art. Working with fibre has always been seen as a woman's craft, never art, and, by extension, a 'lesser' craft. It takes as much skill to weave a tapestry as it does to paint a watercolour, but one rarely finds stitching selling for millions at a London auction house. During the Middle Ages, men formed guilds and training institutions for 'their' art, but stitching was restricted to the domestic realm. Even when the Industrial Revolution came about and mechanical looms replaced handmade fabrics, it was men who profited and finely detailed embroideries ended up being considered 'too feminine' for the emerging suit-wearing, all-male workforce. The art of hand-stitching is making a comeback thanks to high-end design houses and therefore celebrities promoting and showcasing embroidery in their items such as dresses, jackets, jeans, bags and shoes. Growth of online marketplaces such as Etsy allow women with these skills to finally be able to enjoy the fruits of their labour.

---

[8] Cazzola, A. 'Feminist Fibre Art Tracing the History of Feminine Subversion', Academia.edu, 15 January 2017, https://www.academia.edu/30935410/Feminist_Fibre_Art_Tracing_the_History_of_Feminine_Subversion

Crochet

During the lockdown, a crochet expert in our community created a WhatsApp group for those interested in learning and taking on crochet projects that included hair scrunchies, coasters, table runners, scarves and more. The group sent handmade woollen scarves to our soldiers on the Ladakh borders before the onset of the icy-cold winters. The soldiers sent their thanks via a message and a picture, telling the ladies that they wore the woollens every single day and stayed warm. The group continues to knit and crochet useful things for our soldiers in the Indian army. The sense of satisfaction and fulfilment at being able to contribute a wee bit towards caring for the soldiers who guard and protect the country is impossible to express in words.

It is not clear where the origins of crochet lie. According to the Crochet Guild of America website, there are three possibilities. It may have started in Arabia and migrated to the Mediterranean countries. Primitive tribes in South America used crochet ornaments in puberty rituals. Three-dimensional dolls were made from crochet in China.

Historically, crochet-like techniques were employed by men to make nets used for trapping animals, birds and fish. It was also used to make bags to carry the hunted game. Crochet was also used to make adornments for occasions like weddings, funerals and religious rites. It was a poor man's substitute for lace, which was used by sixteenth-century royalty in Europe to adorn their garments.

In Victorian times, crochet moved to everyday objects like tablecloths and flowerpot holders. In the early 1900s, more cosy household objects like rugs, Afghans, cushions, tea-cosies, pot-holders and hot water bottle cases became popular crochet items—all of which contribute to the hygge craze of the current times. Type 'hygge' on Pinterest, and you will find all these cosy crochet accessories for the home. In the 1970s and beyond, crochet was a means of expression, and it could be used to make anything from art to clothing such as blouses, skirts, stoles, etc.

Crochet is minimalistic in its needs and the two main tools needed are a hook and yarn. Hooks can be made from metal, bamboo or plastic and are available in different sizes, which depend on the thickness of the shaft of the hook. Yarn is available in wool, cotton and acrylic, and in different gauges (thickness).

Benefits of Stitching and Needlecraft

- Simple projects like a crocheted throw, handmade kitchen towels, face cloths or bathing scrubs can make time at home a cosier experience. Think hygge.
- All of these are wholesome non-screen-based hobbies.
- Stitching/crochet/knitting are mindful, meditative activities and slow down, heal and calm the hyper anxious mind.
- These activities are well suited to pursuing a sustainable lifestyle.

Natural Dyeing

There are some crafts that I was a silent spectator of for years before diving in, while some entered my life through happenstance. My brush with fabric dyeing at home was one such experience.

During the lockdown, I saw a notice for an interesting Zoom workshop run by Jaishikha Ratanpal, an expert in Indian textiles and costumes, a sustainability enthusiast and a natural dyer. It sounded too good to miss. A three-hour workshop can only spark an interest in a subject and not teach you all of it. This workshop was my window into the world of natural dyes. I also learnt about the harmful effects of chemical dyes on the groundwater, the environment and our own health.

India has a long history of using colourful dyes made from naturally occurring substances. Cotton was used to make fabric as early as 2500 BCE. Ancient India had a culture of drapes. Dhotis, saris with different kinds of draping styles and turbans were all one long piece of cloth used in different ways. Other fibres used for clothing over the years were silk, flax, linen, wool and leather. One of the most iconic statues from the Indus Valley Civilization is the 'Priest King', which shows a man draped in an ornate shawl or robe. Archaeological findings, art (Ajanta and Bagh paintings), caves, sculptures and temples all give an indication of the kind of clothes that were worn in the periods in which the art was made.

The earliest dyed sample of cloth in India was discovered in Mohenjo-Daro, which was dyed with madder root (*manjusha*). India's knowledge and usage of natural dyes goes back to Vedic times. Historically, India's long-standing monopoly in dyed, printed and painted textiles is well known. The knowledge of mordants was well known to the dyers of the Indus Valley Civilization, which was a closely guarded secret. Mordants are agents that react with fugitive dyes (dyes that run colour) and help fix the colour to the fabric. From the fifteenth century onwards, block-printed fabrics from Gujarat and the Deccan were a part of European clothing and upholstery.[9]

Natural Dyes

Natural dyes are obtained from mineral, animal and plant sources. Most natural dyes are derived from different parts of plants such as the root, bark, berries, wood and leaves. Some of these are indigo, madder, turmeric, safflower, pomegranate and myrobalans. Indigo was an important commodity traded and exported from India to Britain. During the British rule over India, these dyes were exported to countries around the world. In the early years, the East India Company gave considerable support to indigo farmers and dye-makers. This was clearly with the selfish intention of increasing production of a material that they could export and make huge profits, seeing the demand in the rest of the world.

---

[9] https://insa.nic.in/writereaddata/UpLoadedFiles/IJHS/Vol17_1_6_HCBhardwaj.pdf

Synthetic Dyes

In 1856, the first synthetic dye was made as a result of
the Industrial Revolution in Europe. The promotional
activities led to greater acceptance of synthetic dyes
in the Indian market. The advantages that synthetic
dyes had over natural dyes were that they were low-
cost, gave a uniform shade and the colour was long-
lasting. The East India Company earned huge profits
by exporting Indian natural dyes to the world and used
these profits to fuel the Industrial Revolution, which in
turn saw the manufacture of chemical dyes that finally
replaced the natural dyes. Filling India with cheaper
dyes made in their industries and factories damaged
the market for indigenous dyes.

Chemical dyes are often harmful for the skin,
cause water pollution, require excessive use of water
to manufacture and thereby harm the environment.
Some of the chemicals used in the dyeing process can
be carcinogenic for the people involved in the industry.

Plant-based and natural dyes, however, are tough to
recreate on a mass scale. They can be used by smaller
businesses and at home with more ease. A lot of foods
and ingredients that, much to our disappointment, end
up staining our whites or sofas, are just the ones that
make very good dyes.

Tea, coffee, flowers including rose, marigold, hibiscus
and bougainvillea, pomegranate peels, turmeric, and
avocado skins and stones are just some of the materials
that can be used to make dyes at home. By employing
simple tie-dye techniques, these home-made dyes can be
used to make wonderful dyed combinations on natural
fabrics.

Some Natural Dyes

Source	Dyed colour	Mordant	Best fabrics
Tea	Off white, cream	Vinegar or alum	Cotton, linen, silk, wool
Coffee	Light to dark brown	Not required	All natural fibres
Turmeric	Yellow, indigo, green	Vinegar	Cotton
Onion skins	Golden yellow	Not required, but alum can be used	Wool, hemp, cotton
Avocado stone and peel	Blush pink	Alum	Cotton, wool, linen
Roses	Light pink to green	Alum	Cotton, linen, hemp, silk

Steps Involved in Natural Dyeing at Home

1. Choosing the fabric

The first step in natural dyeing is to choose the right fabrics. Natural dyes work only on natural fibres, which could be either cellulose-based such as cotton, linen and hemp, or protein-based such as wool and silk.

2. Washing the fabric

Simmering the fabric in soapy water for one to two hours or soaking it overnight followed by rinsing and washing it well ensures that any starch or residues are removed from the fabric. This makes the fabric receptive to the dyeing process.

3. Pre-mordanting

Mordanting is the technique used to make the fibres of the fabric absorb the dye easily. Mordants are the substances used in this process and they fix the colour on the fabric. This process can be done before, during or after the dyeing process. When done before the dyeing process, it is called pre-mordanting.

Without mordanting, these natural dyes will wear off in a few washes. Vinegar and alum are two of the easily available mordants. While these are not essential, the process of natural dyeing is a long one, and mordanting makes the effort worthwhile by making the fabrics retain colour even after numerous washes. Some dyes like tea do fine without mordanting as the tannins in the tea make it stick to the natural fibres.

Alum is a commonly used mordant for most natural dyes. Soak the fabric to be dyed in water with 3 to 4 teaspoons of alum and leave it overnight or else simmer for forty-five minutes.

For more precise measurements, the recommended quantity of alum to be used for mordanting protein fibres like wool and silk is 10 per cent of the weight of the fabric. Some dyers recommend adding cream of tartar to assist the mordant. This helps fix the dye better. Cream of tartar is used as 8 per cent of the weight of the fabric. If the silk or wool (fabric or yarn) weighs 100 g, then 10 g of alum and 8 g of cream of tartar is added to the water in which the fabric is wetted, immersed and simmered or left overnight.

For cellulose fibres (cotton, linen, hemp), the alum used is 25 per cent of the weight of the fabric. For 100 g of fabric, 25 g of alum dissolved in water is used for mordanting.

Turmeric when used as a dye needs vinegar as a pre-mordant. Use one part vinegar in four parts water and immerse the wetted fabric in this overnight or simmer for forty-five minutes.

4. Dye extraction

The next step is to prepare the dye using one of the many natural ingredients that can be used such as turmeric, madder root, rose, tea, coffee, pomegranate peels, avocado stone and peel, etc. Botanicals do better with simmering in a large pot of water for an hour and then soaking in the water overnight. The botanicals can also be soaked in water overnight and then simmered for an hour. A considerable quantity of flowers, leaves or peels are required to extract the dye. If you want to dye a fabric that weighs 100 g, then use a minimum of 100 g of flowers or peels.

5. Dyeing

Now comes the fun part. Dyeing the fabric in your own home-made dye!

- Sieve the prepared natural dye into a large pot. The liquid dye will be collected in the pot and the botanicals will be collected in the sieve. The latter can be discarded into compost. Dilute the collected liquid dye with water so that there is enough liquid for the fabric to be soaked.
- Wet the pre-mordanted fabric and soak it in the pot of dye.
- Simmer for 1 hour.
- Remove with a pair of tongs and rinse under water until the colour no longer runs.
- Dry the fabric in the shade.
- Your home-dyed fabric is ready for use.

6. Post-mordanting

Some natural dyes do better with post-mordanting, which means fixing the colour after the fabric has been dyed. The technique is the same as that outlined in pre-mordanting.

Benefits of Dyeing at Home

Dyeing using botanicals at home is environmentally friendly and provides an outlet to get creative with fabrics and colours.

- Most of the ingredients for natural dyes can be found at home, or can be easily bought. This is a good way to use food waste like peels and stones.
- Getting messy with water and plant-based dyes and spending time with the tying techniques (in case you are doing a tie-and-dye project) makes

it a fun family activity with older kids. They can even make a wall hanging or tablecloth for their room using these techniques.

- The usage of zero chemical dyes in the project is a bonus. Natural dyes are non-toxic, do not pollute water and are safe for the skin.
- You get softer and unusual shades with natural dyes and there is an element of surprise too.
- Homemade tie-dye fabrics make beautiful handmade gifts. A simple piece of tie-dyed cloth makes for a pretty gift wrapping, which can be used in any number of ways by the recipient—right from using it to wrap a gift or a piece of jewellery, to using it as a bandana or a handkerchief.
- Simple whites like kurtas, T-shirts, scarves, dupattas, pillow covers or saris can be dyed and refurbished in these vibrant colours and made more beautiful by incorporating various tie techniques. Tie-dyed fabric pieces can also be used to make kitchen napkins, bandanas, reusable bowl covers or beeswax wraps, face masks and sustainable shopping bags.
- It is one of the non-screen-based hobbies we can indulge in.
- With due experience and expertise, it can be made into a small business.

Interview with Anab Naiyer of Oony by Anab

Anab is an independent maker based out of Delhi. She creates beautiful products using knitting, crochet, embroidery and macramé, which are sold under the brand name Oony by Anab.

Having learnt the crafts from her grandmother, it was the women in her family that inspired her to believe that this could be more than a hobby.

She is on a mission to revive vintage fibre arts in her work and provides DIY kits and tutorials on the same. She is also a full-time PhD student in literature and loves to spend her days making new things in her home and garden.

Tell us about yourself, Anab.

I was born in a very small town in Uttar Pradesh on the Nepal border called Bahraich. We were two sisters and we lived in a big joint family. In this very small town in UP, there were not many things we could do as girls in the nineties. We could either read, help out at home, paint or hang around on the terrace. Out of all the indoor options that I was offered, knitting and crochet especially struck a chord with me, and I took to them. I was eight or nine when I started crochet. Then there was a long hiatus from crochet. When I moved out to attend college, my college friend was into knitting and she's the one who got me back into it.

What forms of thread and crafts do you do and how did you get into them?

Weaving is the basic term for all fibre arts such as knitting, crochet, macramé and embroidery. I started with crochet as it was easy and quick. I am also into knitting and embroidery, which I learnt from my grandma and aunts. Learning one fibre art makes it easy to do the other art forms as it is a dextrous art, but the technique in each art is different. The tactile aspect of each one as well as the kind of product outcomes are very different in each one.

How did you get drawn to handmade fibre arts?

Handmade is an ethical question for me. From the beginning, I have followed the ethic that if I had to choose between machine-made and handmade, I would always choose the latter. In our family, we place a very high value on handmade things. One has to recognize the labour that has gone behind these things. The factory-made products are designed to obliterate the labour that has gone behind it. If I buy something off a rack in a store, the money I pay for the brand goes towards making me oblivious to who stitched the dress, who wove the fabric or where it came from. You don't have to make everything. Even if you make one thing, you will be aware of the skill and value and labour that goes behind it.

Knitting and crochet were always looked upon as something one's granny would do for her grandchildren or as something to keep her hands occupied. Today, they have become a cool millennial thing. What are your thoughts on that?

Grandmothers had one thing that none of us had— time. Post-independence, women have taken the work environment by storm and have done well for themselves. Men do not contribute to domestic affairs, especially in the Indian context. Women don't have time to do home-based jobs like make papads, pickles, crochet, sew, embroider, etc., any more.

Old women doing sedentary activities in their leisure time like knitting or crochet is neither respected as a skill nor labour, which is a big reason why these crafts are not valued. It is just counted as an act of love. As there are not too many of those grandmothers around us in present times, people are realizing the value of these handmade items. It is turning into a valued business.

It is difficult to explain to people how to pay for a handmade article because they feel like their grandmother did it for free out of love. South Asian women are very talented but not recognized for their talent as they have been giving it all away for nothing.

A full-size sweater takes fifty to sixty hours to make, which a grandmother would make out of love for her grandchildren. You cannot put a cost on handmade items.

Do you find a connection between using your hands for these crafts and mental wellness?

Knitting is called mental yoga for a reason as it brings concentration to the mind and rhythm to your hands. It is difficult to gather your thoughts when your hands are not occupied. Due to the repetition and not having to think about what I'm going to do next, I can take a problem that's on hand and think about it while knitting without getting distracted. Distraction stunts our intellect and perspective in a huge way. Knitting and crochet offer windows of time to think, which is a luxury.

There is an unnecessary gender stereotyping attached to these crafts. Schools teach boys to knit these days to improve hand-eye coordination and fine motor skills, and I find that to be a welcome change. What are your thoughts on this?

Men who knit and crochet are very few. There is a huge bias. Men are affected by patriarchy as much as women. Younger kids in schools getting into these handmade crafts is a good start. There is a long way to go for this to become a categorically gender-neutral activity.

For a complete newbie, what are the crafts in needle/ thread work he/she can get started with?

Macramé is the easiest as it is just knotting, and no other tools are required. Embroidery is also easy, and it just requires practice. We are intimidated by many crafts as they are expensive to learn and to do. None of these fibre arts are expensive, unlike other crafts. Women in small towns and villages are still able to afford doing these fibre arts like embroidery, either for their leisure or for themselves or their children.

What's the best way to learn one of these crafts?

Talk to your neighbours or aunts. You will surely find some of them well versed with the craft and they will be happy to teach you.

The second most valuable resource is YouTube, which has innumerable tutorials.

What is the scope of converting this hobby into a business? Do share your own personal experience with this.

I started my business on social media and my website will be up soon. The problem with a handmade craft business is that making a steady income from it is a very long journey. There are a number of guides for marketing and pricing in the West for handmade goods, as they lack free labour in the family.

When I started in late 2017, I was making everything myself, but the following year I could not go on like that. One product takes a few days to make. Making each product by hand and selling it is not good enough for a stable income; it is not scalable. Always price the product well, don't sell it for cheap. That devalues your skill, your time and the whole handmade industry. People get used to getting handmade stuff for cheap, which takes the whole market down. For the last year and a half, there has been a growing market and audience who are interested in handmade, and who want to learn more about it. You need to make people understand that x number of hours went into the making of a product, which is why it is worth the price. When you start respecting the skill behind the product, that's when you have a transaction that is beneficial to the maker and the buyer.

What's the one project someone can do in a couple of hours?

Cotton scrubbies to scrub and wash your face is a quick and nice project, and they are ready in fifteen minutes. They are sustainable and reusable, and you can make a set of six to use for the whole week, wash them on Sunday and then the whole set is ready for the next week.

Projects

1. Tea-Dyed Tea Towel   297
2. Rose-Dyed Handkerchiefs   298
3. Reusable Bowl Covers   300
4. All-Natural Scent Sachets and Heating Pads   301
5. Crochet Hair Scrunchies   303
6. Crochet Dishcloths   306

1. Tea-Dyed Tea Towel

This project uses CTC tea leaves available in most Indian kitchens to dye fabrics. The tannins in the tea fix the dye to the fabric and no mordanting (treatment to fix the colour to the fabric) is needed.

Read the note on the step-by-step process of natural dyeing given earlier in the chapter before getting started.

Gather

Detergent / soap
2 plain white tea towels in pure cotton or linen
2 dozen small rubber bands
Large steel pot
4 tbsp tea leaves (CTC)

Make

Washing: Before getting on with the dyeing, soak the cotton towels in soap water overnight. Wash well and dry. This is to remove all traces of starch from the fabric. This can be done on the previous day or days before starting the dyeing process.

Preparing the dye: On the day of dyeing, fill the pot with enough water to immerse the towels. Add the tea and keep the water to boil for fifteen minutes to extract all the colour. Let the tea leaves sit in the liquid until you are ready to start the dyeing process.

Tying the fabric: Using any of the easy tie-dye techniques you can find on YouTube, apply the rubber bands tightly in places around the pre-washed tea towel.

Dyeing: Strain the tea leaves and discard. Keep the brewed and strained tea in the pot. Wet the fabrics and add to the pot. Simmer on a low flame for forty-five minutes.

Rinsing: Rinse these well until no colour runs out. Remove the rubber bands and dry the cloth in shade.

Your tea-dyed tie-dye tea towels are ready. Tea gives an off-white to light brown vintage colouring to the fabric.

Notes: You can skip the tie-dye and keep it as a plain dyed tea towel too.

You can also use this technique to give an antique or vintage look to a faded white tablecloth or to lace doilies. It's also a great way to tie-dye a white vest or T-shirt.

2. Rose-Dyed Handkerchiefs

Roses give the most beautiful colours to natural fibres from pink to light green. The colour also depends on the colour of the roses used, the darker red roses giving a darker colour than the light pink or peach roses. Although handkerchiefs have gone out of style, let us give paper towels a miss and get back to the sustainable practice of carrying our handkerchief, be it to wipe sweat or our hands.

Read the note on the step-by-step process of natural dyeing given earlier in the chapter before getting started.

Gather

4 plain white cotton handkerchiefs
⅓ cup vinegar
20 red or pink roses
1 lemon

Make

Some of these processes can be done simultaneously such as pre-mordanting and preparing the dye.

Washing: Soak the handkerchiefs in soapy water overnight to get rid of any starch. Wash well.

Pre-mordanting: Mix ⅓ cup vinegar with 1 cup water. Soak the washed handkerchiefs in this solution overnight. Rinse and wash well.

Prepare the dye: Pluck out the petals of the roses. For one part rose petals, take two parts water. Combine the two in a pan and simmer for forty-five minutes. Let this sit overnight to extract maximum pigment. Pass through a sieve into a large pot, squeezing out all the liquid from the petals. This is the dye. Squeeze lemon juice into this. Dilute with some water as required so that the handkerchiefs to be dyed are fully immersed in this liquid.

Dyeing: Wet the pre-mordanted handkerchiefs and add them to the pot with the rose extract. Simmer for forty-five minutes or leave overnight.

Rinsing: Remove and rinse under water until the colour no longer runs. Squeeze and dry in the shade.

Your rose-dyed handkerchiefs are ready for use.

Note: For an added adornment, get roses embroidered on the corner of each handkerchief.

3. Reusable Bowl Covers

Fabric-based bowl covers are useful to keep bowls covered in the fridge or on the counter, instead of using cling wrap. These look like fabric shower caps but made for bowls and baskets. They are great for covering dough kept on the counter in bowls, be it atta for rotis or while making yeasted breads or sourdough. These are washable and reusable. They are not airtight so they may not be good to cover food bowls kept in the fridge for longer durations, but they work well for three to four hours.

Gather

Round pieces of washed cotton fabric in three different sizes depending on what size bowls you usually use for refrigeration/storage, etc. You can take the bowl for which you want to make the cover to measure the size of the cloth. Place the bowl upside down on the cloth and draw a circle 2 inches outside the circumference of the bowl.

Measuring tape or bowls to measure cloth size
Pen or fabric marker
6–7 pins (options)
Needle and thread or sewing machine
A roll of ¼ inch elastic
Safety pin

Make

Cut the cloth into circles using the bowls as a reference. Keep the cloth right side down.

Fold half an inch all around the circumference of the circle and secure with pins if required. Sow the folded part all around, leaving a 1-inch gap to insert the elastic piece.

The length of elastic cord required is 4–5 inches less than the circumference of the bowl. Measure and cut a length of the elastic cord accordingly.

Insert a safety pin at one end of the elastic cord. Thread the elastic using the safety pin through the opening in the stitch and push it all through the stitched tunnel at the circumference of the cloth. Once the elastic comes out from the other end of the opening, stitch the two ends of the elastic together by hand or machine.

Lastly, stitch the opening by hand. The reusable bowl cover is ready.

4. All-Natural Scent Sachets and Heating Pads

Use these scent sachets in the car, wardrobes, sock drawers and shoe cabinets. Other spaces where these aroma sachets work well are laundry baskets, in the garbage area, the entryway of the house and in bathrooms. Instead of buying chemical and artificial scent-filled sprays or diffusers, these work beautifully. Camphor pieces in these sachets leave a nice aroma, infinitely better than naphthalene balls.

Gather

A few leftover pieces of fabric, old dupattas or T-shirts, cut into 3×6" pieces—gather as many such pieces as you want to make sachets. Use breathable cotton or muslin.

To fill:

Raw rice grains
Camphor crystals / Essential oils / Lavender buds

Make

In a bowl, mix the rice along with one of the three given options, either camphor, essential oil or lavender buds.

For ¼ cup of rice, use ¼ cup camphor crystals or 10 drops of essential oil, or use 2 parts lavender buds to 1 part rice by volume. Mix well and keep aside.

Fold each fabric piece in half along the short side on the reverse. Stitch one short end and one long end with two rows of running stitches.

The open end is the opening of the sachet. Fold a 3-cm flap down towards the reverse side. Make a ½-cm fold towards the inside and hem this for a neat finish.

Fill the sachet with the prepared stuffing and secure it tightly with a rubber band. You can knot another rubber band around this to use as the hanger. To make it resemble farmhouse chic, tie a jute cord around the rubber band on the neck.

Another option is to pass a cord around the hemmed top fold and leave a small opening for you to be able to pull the cord and tie it tightly after the sachet is filled with the material.

You can also stuff the scented filling and stitch to seal the opening, to use these sachets in drawers, but these are not easily refilled once the scents have evaporated.

Heating Pads

Make around 6- to 8-inch square bags with cotton material, keeping one end open. Fill with rice and eucalyptus essential oil and seal the open side with running stitches after filling the bag. These can be microwaved for a minute or two and used as heating pads for any aches and pains. These also make for lovely gifts.

For all crochet projects, do look up single crochet, slip stitch and double crochet stitch video tutorials online. They are much easier when learnt through a video than via text. Crochet patterns are often written down for magazines or websites and once you know the basic stitches and terminologies it is easy to follow the pattern like a pro.

5. Crochet Hair Scrunchies

This is the quickest crochet project you can do and that too by learning just a couple of basic stitches. If you are like me and keep losing your scrunchies all around the house or if your bags seem to swallow the scrunchies, you'll love making these for yourself in a variety of colours and patterns. Using a thick yarn bulks up the scrunchie quickly while using thinner yarn may take extra time. They also make for pretty and useful gifts for friends and family with long hair. These are also gentler on the hair than thin rubber bands.

Gather

Good quality plain hair rubber bands
Yarn—cotton/wool/mixed material in any colour you like
Crochet needle depending on the yarn used
Scissors

Make

Do look up single crochet, slip stitch and double crochet stitch video tutorials online before getting started.

Take the free end of the yarn and make a knot around the rubber band.

First row:

Insert the crochet hook into the rubber band, take the yarn over and pull through. Do another yarn over and pull through both the loops. This is a single crochet. Continue doing this until you cover the entire circumference of the rubber band.

When this stage is reached, do a slip stitch to join with the end where you started the first stitch.

Second row:

1. Do a chain 3 (3 chain stitches)
2. Now do a double crochet, for which you do a yarn over, insert the hook under the V at the same place where you took the chain stitches, yarn over and pull through. At this point, you will have 3 loops on the crochet hook. Pull through two loops which will leave you with one loop on the hook. Do another yarn over and pull through two loops, which will leave you with one loop on the hook. This completes one double crochet. Do another double crochet in the same stitch spot.
3. Now onward do 3 double crochets in every stitch until you reach the 3 chain stitch point where you started.
4. To join, do a slip stitch at the base of the V of the third chain stitch, cut the yarn, leaving around 2 to 3 inches length, and pull it through the two loops, tightening the knot. This free yarn can be woven into the gap to finish the scrunchie.

This is one of the few methods to make an easy scrunchie.

A faster method is to go around the entire circumference of the rubber band doing triple crochets directly around the band without the base single crochets outlined in the method above. This is much faster and uses less yarn as it needs only one row of crochet. Look up videos on how to do triple crochet.

6. Crochet Dishcloths

These make for sustainable wiping cloths. Combine with a handmade dishwashing soap and a coir brush for a lovely gift to someone who appreciates sustainable and handmade. A good idea suggested by Anab Naiyar from Oony by Anab is to make six, one for each of the six days of the week, and wash them all on the seventh day. Use 100 per cent cotton yarn for this project.

7 inches square is a good size for these dishcloths.

Gather

100 per cent cotton yarn (medium thickness)
Crochet hook

Make

Start with a slip knot on the hook and make 30 chain stitches. The number of stitches will depend on the thickness of the yarn. You can measure a 7" length of the chain before proceeding to the second row.

For the second row, start doing a single crochet into each stitch, starting from the second stitch.

To start the third row, do a chain one (one chain stitch) and turn the project over to repeat the same process as the second row. Continue doing this row after row until you get a square or a piece of a size you want.

End the last stitch with a knot, cut off the yarn and weave the loose end inside.

Note: Doing this with multicolour yarn gives a nice effect to the dishcloth.

You can crochet a thin ribbon and stitch it like a loop to one corner if you want to hang the dishcloth from a hook.

Chapter 9

The Business of Handmade

'He who works with his hands is a labourer.
He who works with his hands and his head
is a craftsman.
He who works with his hands and his head and his
heart is an artist.'
—St Francis of Assisi

How often does it happen that you are good at something and family and friends egg you on to take it more seriously than just a hobby? This could be cooking, crafts, home decor or anything else. Taking a passion to a professional level is a huge leap. Let us run through some of the elements involved in this journey.

Before You Get into Business

Pros and cons

It's a good first step to make a note of the pros and cons of converting your hobby into a business. This reality check will help you take a well thought out decision.

Pros	Cons
Doing what you love	Need to learn/do a lot more things than just your hobby
Being your own boss	What was done for fun is now work
Deciding your work hours	Starting afresh and losing your main income
Added income if doing it as a side hustle	Loss of company-paid health insurance and other benefits

Write down in detail why you want to convert your hobby into a business.

- Is it to work full time on something you love doing?
- Would you rather be doing this instead of your job?
- What problem is it going to solve for your customers?
- Is your hobby making enough money for you as a side hustle?

Identify your ideal customer

Always know who the customer is that you are catering to. In the times of social-media marketing, it is important to nail this to the T so that your business can be marketed to this specific group of people. Unlike newspapers and magazines, in digital media, companies know the customer profile better than the customers themselves, so make use of this.

Age, gender, income, occupation, location, marital status/life stage, psychographics (attitudes, beliefs, hobbies, interests), what are their goals, what influences their buying decisions, what do they read, preferred social media—this is some of the data with which you can define your ideal customer. Some businesses prefer to collect this information when you sign up for their website or when you make a first purchase.

Market research

- *Customer research*: Market research helps narrow down what your customer wants. Use free services like Google Forms or Survey Monkey to design forms that can collect all the information you need. Share the link to the form among your family and friends via WhatsApp groups, asking them to forward the form to more groups so you can gather a fair number of responses. The results get tabulated in the backend and it gives you all the information at-a-glance.

- *Competitor research*: Research the products, the marketing and social media strategies of brands you consider to be competitors. You can emulate the winning strategies of competitors while improving on their weaknesses. Try to devise a better product and customer experience than what is offered by your competitors.

Business plan

Even if you don't have a degree in business, it is important to draw out a business plan for your handmade business. There are several tutorials on YouTube that will guide you on how to make one. If the process is too intimidating, then enlist the help of a relative or friend with a background in business management to help you make the business plan. Some of the aspects in a business plan are the executive summary, a detailed description of your business, competitor and market analysis, SWOT (strengths, weaknesses, opportunities, and threats) analysis, marketing and sales plan, and financial projections. A business plan is vital when you are looking for external funding.

Once You Decide to Get into Business

Find your USP

While you may have a broad idea of what line of business you want to be in, such as baking, pickle-making or jewellery-making, it is best to narrow down to one particular niche and answer the question 'What problem am I solving?' to bring something unique to the market. For example: baking with zero refined ingredients and added sugars, suitable for diabetics and health-conscious people, or making jewellery with recycled materials. This not only helps grab attention because of your unique business idea but also helps draw a clear customer profile, which makes it easier when it comes to marketing.

Treat it like a full-time job

Family, friends and neighbours tend to take your availability for granted if you are working for yourself or from home. Right from the start, you should decide your working hours so that all other chores are completed before you settle in your work area with a do-not-disturb attitude. Working for yourself does allow some degree of flexibility, but that should be the exception and not the rule. As someone who works as a writer from home, I have had neighbours invite me for weekday lunches saying I can always get my work done later. I rarely accept an unscheduled invite when I have deadlines as it means I will have to work late or on weekends to compensate for an unexpected break from my writing hours. This also means you need to have a proper morning routine of waking up at a certain time, figuring out time for chores, exercise, etc., so you can show up at your desk at the same time every day.

Treat it like a proper business

Get your business a name, tagline and a logo. Brainstorm with friends who are creative with this sort of thing or into advertising. Keep the name simple, searchable and easy to remember. Remember that everything should be Google search-friendly as an online presence is vital in the current times. If you are a healthy baking brand, then make sure the terms 'healthy baking' feature in the brand name or the tagline for better discovery. At the same time, don't let the name limit your business drastically as you may want to expand to other product lines in the future. Outsource the legal work like registering the business and trademark, and any tax-related paperwork like GST to a competent chartered accountancy or law firm.

Be money-wise

Check your current financial situation, calculate the amount required to start and keep the business running, and figure out any other liabilities, insurance requirements, etc., depending on whether you're going to start it as a side hustle or a full-time business. It is always recommended to not quit your current job while testing the waters of 'hobbypreneurship'. It helps keep the boat afloat while also helping you fund your new business. This will no doubt require a lot of extra hours of work put in, but it is the lowest risk option. If there is backing from family or an early investor, then you may consider quitting and working on your business idea.

Set goals

It's always easier to work towards a goal. Be it allocating hours of work, personnel, investing in materials and so on. Goals could be long term or short term. They could be production goals (for example: creating 300 pieces of beeswax wraps in one month), sales goals (selling 100 cakes in a month) or social-media goals (increasing follower count on Instagram by 500 in a month). Keep the goals realistic, flexible and scalable.

Update/upgrade your skills

The biggest difference between pursuing a hobby and making it a business is that you're no longer just baking cakes or making kombucha. You have to make the transition from being master of the creative process to Jill/Jack of all trades. In addition to the creative work, there will be extra administrative work, dealing with vendors and suppliers, managing public relations and marketing, copywriting, becoming a social-media ninja, a spreadsheet expert, a finance expert, a photographer, a video editor and lots more. Some of this may come naturally to you and some other stuff may be utter drudgery. Initially, it is a good idea to rope in family and friends who are good at each of these roles to pitch in so that you are not overwhelmed by too many things at once. Eventually, you will figure out what it is you are good at, what your kids can be bribed to do for you and what you may need to outsource. Using freelancers and online services like Fiver (where any service can be outsourced for US$5) is a good way to save money on these services. Legal and financial aspects need to be ironclad, so do hire the best help you can get in these departments.

In the online space, your product is only as good as its description and photograph. So make sure both of these are top notch.

Pursue short courses in areas like writing, photography and editing to upgrade your skills to be able to sell your products. Many of these courses are available for free on YouTube or Coursera and on many other sites for a reasonable fee.

Get the required permissions

If you will be running the business from home, make sure the valid licences are in place. Kombucha or fermented drinks may have a small percentage of alcohol. Check with knowledgeable local people who can guide you if any special licences need to be procured for such businesses. You may also need to disclose to your housing society if your home address is being used to run a business. Such rules differ from state to state. It is best to seek the advice of similar business owners in your vicinity. Selling food items requires a permission called FSSAI. The initial paperwork and licence procuring may feel like a hassle, but it is of utmost importance so your business does not run into problems later.

Packaging and design

Standout packaging and design can add to your USP and be a talking point when it comes to word-of-mouth marketing. In the times before Indigo Airlines, all airlines had the same dreary packaging for food served on air. Indigo made their packaging stand out and used whacky copywriting, which was definitely one of the talking points about the food, as there's only so much improvement one can make to the airline food itself.

Pricing your product

Quite often, handmade business owners are confused about how to price their product. Another mistake they make is to underestimate the value of their product and price it rather low. Getting the pricing right is very important so that your business makes a profit and is sustainable. Product pricing is not just adding a small margin to the cost of materials. It needs to include time cost, design and production of packaging cost, cost of marketing, taxes and a lot more. Take your time to work out a number that takes into consideration all of these. There is also the perceived value of a product you are selling. If your brand sells luxury candles and your pricing of Rs 250 covers all of the above but your targeted customer easily pays Rs 500 per similar candle, then you could be pricing your product at Rs 500.

Marketing Your Business

Social media

The Internet has enabled businesses to run from any corner of India and cater to the rest of the country. I have bought pottery from Gujarat, plants from Manipur and snacks from a town in Tamil Nadu via Instagram. This is the magic of doing social media right. As soon as you finalize the name for your business, make sure to get the corresponding URL for a website and handles on Instagram, Facebook, Twitter, etc. You can decide later which platforms will be the focus for marketing, but it's good to have all of these at your disposal. It is not a bad idea to see what names are easily available on these platforms and then choose the business name accordingly. Don't use these platforms purely to sell. Tell your story, follow your dream customers, start conversations, make connections and sales will follow. Utilize all that each platform has to offer—for example, Live on Facebook and Instagram, Instagram Reels and Stories, Spaces on Twitter and so on. Understand what kind of content will be relevant to your audience and create this on the go.

An Indian ethnic-wear brand called Indian EthnicCo used Reels on Instagram; they posted thirty-second dance videos to catchy songs with the dancers wearing the clothes of their brand. Each of these videos would go viral. They are possibly the only brand to be featured by Instagram itself, causing their popularity to skyrocket. It's often a simple idea used at the right time that can go viral, bringing you tons of customers and business, so it is important to keep trying.

Pinterest

Pinterest is not included in the social-media section as it is essentially a visual search engine. Most handmade things, be it sourdough or spice mixes or soaps, have a rustic beauty about them, which if captured well in photographs can be the biggest driving force in their marketing. Using these images on your website or a third-party shopping website and pinning these images to Pinterest with relevant keywords and search engine optimization (SEO) could boost discovery, visibility and sales. It is worthwhile taking a course on how Pinterest works and how to leverage it to the maximum for your business.

Blog

Even though blogging seems very yesteryearly, it's not to be dismissed entirely. Having content relevant to your business in a blog with properly done SEO can bring a lot of customers to your website via Google searches. While this could be outsourced, no one knows the intricacies of your brand and business like you do, so it's best if you write this yourself or at least provide all the content to the writers. Keep the blog updated and current. If your brand is about healthy baking, then look out for tentpole events like World Health Day, World Diabetes Day, World Chocolate Day, etc., to create content around these topics. You can also regularly share simple recipes and tips around healthy baking, thereby providing value-added content to your followers and not just using the platform to sell all the time.

Newsletter

All your content on social media depends on the platform showing your content to the public. A change in algorithm or an overnight ban (TikTok in

India) or the platform itself losing steam means you lose the customer base you've built there over the years. In addition to having a social-media presence, it is important to have a newsletter going out to your customers, existing and potential. It enables you to have direct access to your customer's mailbox. Keep the content interesting with offers thrown in from time to time and you can be sure that they will be opening your newsletter to read it. All new visitors to your website can be given the option to share their email ID for purposes of a newsletter or offer emails in exchange for a discount coupon code.

Live events

In 2020–21, we have almost forgotten about and written off live events, with nearly every activity moving to the digital medium. It is not, however, always going to be that way. I have personally discovered a lot of beautiful handmade brands via local events and exhibitions, and these have gone on to become big stores or brands in the coming years. In a live event, it is not just about people buying your product on display. It is a space to interact personally with your potential customers. Giving them a pamphlet or a card or taking their email ID to add to your newsletter mailing list is a way to draw in a customer base in that locality. Think of each such customer as a possible word-of-mouth advertiser for you. Giving away a voucher to all those visiting your stall could also allow them to browse your website or Instagram at leisure and make their purchases in the near future. Such events help put a face to the brand and are a very useful brand-building exercise.

Influencer marketing

Do your research and find influencers who are the best match for your brand. Have a proper contract that covers the deliverables, deadlines and the commercials for the campaign. Request for statistics and sales from their previous campaigns. Look beyond influencers with very high following. Some micro-influencers who have high engagement can be better for your brand, reaching out to your desired audience at a more reasonable cost.

Where to Sell

Online

There are different avenues to sell handmade products online. Your brand's website, social-media platforms like Instagram and Facebook Marketplace, websites like Etsy, Amazon Karigar, Authindia, Craftsvilla and Kreate (through their app) are some of the options. Brands can also sell via e-commerce marketplaces like Shopify.

Offline

Handmade products can be stocked in relevant brick-and-mortar stores, boutiques, organic and wellness stores. Putting up stalls in popups and exhibitions helps not just sales but also visibility and brand building among the target audience.

Wholesaler

Selling products from your own website is a better option for bulk orders. You can create separate registrations, order forms and pricing for bulk buyers. Offer an option for connecting via email or phone to enquire about customization, courier charges and so on.

A hobby is done purely for fun. When you make it a business, some of that fun is bound to get converted into the stress of reaching your goals and deadlines. Don't wait for perfection. In a hobby-to-business landscape, a lot of things will be learnt on the go. Other than your craft, it is not feasible to have complete knowledge or perfection in other departments. Just get started and you will find things falling into place. Your focus should be on doing things to the best of your ability and not the best in the industry.

Whatever you do, make sure your focus is on good quality. That is the one thing that is sure to get you word-of-mouth recommendations and repeat customers. For example, in baking, use the best-quality ingredients and follow the same process every time to get consistent results. This will make you excel in the process. Start with a small menu and focus on getting those three or four items to an excellent quality before focusing on too many. The same could apply to any business.

Starting and running your own business, no matter how small, is an exciting journey. Think of each day as an adventure and a learning opportunity. Accept all the help that comes your way from family and friends until you find your bearings and the funds to outsource to professionals. Network with others from the handmade community. There is a lot to learn from each other's experiences. And, most of all, don't forget the joy you derive from the creative process which is why you got into this in the first place.

Acknowledgements

My publisher at Penguin Random House India, Milee Ashwarya, for seeing this book through to its present form.

Aarushi Singhal, Anab Naiyer, Anita Tikoo, Mallika Basu, Meenakshi Arun, Payal Shah, Pooja Dhingra and Soma Datta for sharing their experiences and expertise.

My late maternal grandparents who nurtured the maker in me since childhood.

Roshini Dadlani and Nicholas Rixon for being part of the book in its early stages.